Breaking Open
the Heart

Collected Works
2009-2017

Gregory David Done

Albion
Andalus
Boulder, Colorado
2017

*"The old shall be renewed,
and the new shall be made holy."*
— Rabbi Avraham Yitzhak Kook

Albion-Andalus, Inc.
P. O. Box 19852
Boulder, CO 80308
www.albionandalus.com

Cover design by Sam Krezinski

Design and layout by Albion-Andalus Books

Manufactured in the United States of America

ISBN-13: 978-0692932469 (Albion-Andalus Books)

ISBN-10: 0692932461

For

Liu Ming & Dharma Bodhi

CONTENTS

I am asleep and dreaming...

Breaking Open the Heart

Clothed in facts,
Truth feels oppressed,
in the garb of poetry
it moves easy and free
—Tagore

ALL WRITING AND talking about life, about god, about enlightenment, attempts to pin down and catch hold of Reality with words, with symbols. But alas, this cannot be done. For Reality is alive— changing, moving, breathing, dying, and cannot be contained in concepts, ideas, or words. We cannot describe Reality, nor can we explain it; it is unspeakable. Life is not a problem to be solved but a reality to be experienced.

After years of reading spiritual and religious literature, and after nearly twenty years of practicing meditation, I have finally discovered, to my chagrin and delight, that there are no answers in books or in words. After all my searching, I find myself in a desert, content to be lost, yet still thirsting for real and direct experience, something words and books cannot provide.

The desert I find myself in is beyond language and beyond ideas, a place without reference points, where all "truth" escapes my grasp as soon as I catch hold of it. The more I drop my stories, relax my reference points, and rest in humility, awe, and wonder, the more I understand, now, that direct experience is the essence of the contemplative life—to understand fully that no matter what you do, you cannot know, you cannot explain, you cannot answer the great riddle of life, the mystery of the universe, for all explanations are relative concepts empty of inherent meaning.

The highest wisdom, it turns out, is the discovery that you know nothing.

When you discover this "nothing" you step out of the symbolic world and into the real one. Emptiness, then, becomes full of magical displays, and everything is revealed as a phantasm of Light, cyclical self-resolving movement, an ever-present naturalness. The fruition of this discovery is wonder.

Resting in wonder, you begin truly to see this mystery, to live in it, to dwell in it, to experience the nature of Reality directly for yourself. Only then does language find its true purpose—to describe the indescribable, to say what cannot be said. Only when we let go of words and concepts are we finally responsible enough to use them.

For me, poetry expresses the pinnacle of language because it makes no sense. If poetry made sense it would not express Reality, for Reality does not make sense. Reality, the ineffable source, the unnamable Way, the awareness-energy that is everything, is pure babbling nonsense. So then, the task of the poet is to dwell in "don't know," to rest in wonder, in awe, and to ride the crest and the trough of the wave of life and through our language channel that babbling source with the beauty of our words through our visceral lived experience.

Every poem is a work of art, a moment in time, a shining jewel of truth. Each poem here is a teardrop shed from the desert of experience that lies beyond language and ideas, a place that every pilgrim on the spiritual path must enter on their journey home, back to the spiritual source.

Anyone who has dared to penetrate their inner silence and stillness will understand that in the matter of truth, silence makes more sense than a lot of words, but if words must be used, then poetry makes more sense than logical prose. Poetry allows us to drink from the nectar of divine life, the Natural State. Everything else attempts to catch water in a sieve, to put legs on a snake.

Poetry, for me, has been an indispensable tool for processing and shedding limiting self-concepts through a kind of symbolic digestion. I stew in my confusion, in my raw open feelings, and then let them speak. Poetry helps me release the natural confusion that comes from integrating non-dual experience with the dual world.

These poems were written during the strange and confusing decade we call our "20's," and their subject is my humanity—my inspiration and my broken heart. I have spent my 20's breaking open my heart, and these poems are what came out. I have ordered them chronologically backwards, beginning with the present, from the fountain of origins. I hope you find something of your humanity in my words.

Thank you very much for reading this work.

May All Beings Be Free!!!

Gregory David Done
Fire Rooster Year

Part I
Red Dust

2015-2017

Everything is Red Dust.

DUST IS THE temporary, compound condition or legacy of our many lifetimes and ancestors. It appears as a substance that makes up the phantom world and the phantom that perceives/ experiences that world. Why is it Red? It is our compulsion to DO (make effort), it is in our blood, in our desires and passions, and it is hot. We are imagining and sensing a hot wind, driven up into a spiral—full of red dust that stings the sky.

—Liu Ming

Dreaming

Wide awake asleep,
Winding through
Wide open landscapes,
Where heart flowers bloom
       With reckless wonder,
       Where Earth goes to
            Water
       And the Five Eyes
Open to spirits, to worlds
       Within worlds,
To the dream of others,
       Here, dreaming
The dirt ball, mud pellet, skin bag
       Sits alone,
Facing a wall, entering
       In to complete I

Don't know

Great Doubt

       Heart giggles,
Clear mind, great doubt
       —don't know.
The impulse persists, and
I have followed it
       Nowhere,

Adulthood spent
Constructing—no value

        I chased my tail
And found the edge
Of the world; bored,
I left only to find
The impulse again

Boundaries burst
        —don't know.
30 turns, and I know
Nothing of what I am
Stamping my feet
I scream into crystal clarity,
And space echoes back
        —don't know.

Air and Light

        Liberating our ghosts,
Emptying the hells, in every step,
With open arms, smiling,
In shameless generosity—
With one human gesture,
Open the gate of freedom wide,
And generations of burden
        Turn to air and light,
Flowers blooming
In the footprints behind us

Great Completion

What is fate?
Other than freedom

Knowing now the story
      Of great completion
Having seen space open,
Full of luminous filaments,
An endless process, compounded,
Filled, also, with innumerable
Ghosts, demons, stories unfinished,
Unresolved, and my own story
Still resolving

     I see, now,
The greatest limitation
Is actually our perfect freedom

We curse fate and beg
     For choice
And at every turn, we
Use our choices
To generate problems
So that we can, in turn,
     Destroy them
With our aggression

And so, we haunt ourselves
And each other, running
In endless circles, hallucinating

That we exist, that we abide
That we should be something
Other than exactly what we are
Somewhere outside, somewhere
Beyond, somewhere better than
The situation we are actually in

The natural state does not prefer
      Enlightenment
Nor does it prefer salvation, or
      Birth over death
And our fate is nothing other than
The situation we find ourselves in
      Right now
Self-generated and self-resolving,
And yet no self to be found, only
A process of freedom
      Choosing limitation
Preferring this over that,
Invoking fear from of an endless
      Phantasm of light

Relaxing into luminous space,
The great completion reveals
Its greatness in the fact
That it is already complete

No self, no problem
Nowhere to go, nothing to become
No one to blame, nothing to
Transform, nothing to improve

This—is the cosmic joke
Nothing can be right
In a universe, where
Nothing can be wrong

Knowing nothing
Of my original nature—
  I do nothing
And hear the eternal
Laughter of the universe,
Echoing in the sound of waves

Dance

  Ascending,
  Reflecting upon
  This, immaculate
Mirror; all emotions
  Arise to
Dance their completion,
Contract and liberate,
Flower into freedom
Love embraces, and facets
  Open, rivers churn
Channels, back to source,
  Descending,
Displaying the external
  Within itself around
Nothing goes anywhere
And I dance a sky pattern

Of laughter on strings
Of marrow and light

Ancestors

This very body—
A mausoleum of ghosts,
A lineage blessing,
    A living gate
To the living universe

Great Emperor Star
The mandate of fate
    Is clear
Spilling over from vast
    Purple oceans
Of fate and luck
To live through me,
Opening a wisdom door
To the open secret

For years, I have wandered,
Alternating characters
Blind to this gift—
    Born human
    Born healthy
    Born free
Emerging from death,
A shining radiance

Of eternal blood and
       Ancestral water

Loved from inception
Cradled in the celestial arms
Of the Great Matriarch
I bow to you—Ancestors
For you are this body, and
Everything I am I inherit
       From you
This eternal procession
Glows in me, an expression
       Of the great rhythm
The dance of planets
The twinkling of stars

With gratitude I accept all of you
My precious ghosts
My worrisome demons
You are liberated, for
I vow to empty every last hell,
Every confusion, every story
       Unresolved

Nothing really dies, for the dead
Live in each body, impure
       Yet immortal
Compounds of emptiness and light

My story is yours,
May we cultivate the Way
And open this living door

Returning to the Land of Ghosts

The heart led me here
The heart leads me back

Dreams lay scattered about
The sand, and my hopes
    Are old trash
Flittering in the ocean air

The beach is littered with
Old hope and modern decadence
Wireless dreams—half dreamed

I sigh and breathe out
The heaviness of youthful fantasy
And turn my eyes back "home"
To the land of ghosts

    Resolved, now,
    To stop dreaming

Calm and clear, I
Follow my heart
To nowhere other
    Than here,

Through now, the gateless gate
To the ordinary life
Where the eternal
Procession flows

All Too Profound

Endless search,
Peeling the onion,
Veil after veil, revealing
Nothing but veils
　　　Behind veils

　　　The great accent
　　　To Truth
Climbing the lonely mountain
Step after step, stage after stage
Transforming, improving,
Revealing the cloudless summit

Great discipline, self-mastery
Conquering the ego...I'm sorry
　　　—too profound;
　　　I dropped my keys

The true Self, the Real You
Eternal Consciousness, bliss,
The One behind the many
　　　I'm sorry...

A little too profound
For this dunce

I peeled the onion—
But it was empty

My Buddha-Nature
Is horny, and it's
Windy again this morning

Hearing God speak,
I could care less

Unless God can tell me
Where the potatoes are,
I think I'll keep wandering

Looking inside, I ask—
But who is looking?
Finding only looking
I can't stop laughing

WHO AM I?
Echoes in space...

WHY AM I HERE?
I'm hungry again...

This is it
The path comes to an end
Amongst the parsley

Yĭ Hài

Falling to the earth,
Filled with praise,
  Tears fall,
And deep relaxation
   Pulses within
Worries flow out, and
Warmth oriels from
The central gate—
  Blown open

I found it again, something
  I thought lost

This matrix of tension
This ancient demon
Has crossed over and out

And beneath the pressure
Beneath the mud, home
Bubbles forth, whispering,
"I am not lost; I never left"

Once revealed, we must find
Our way back; again and again;
  Once home,
We find we out we never left

Perfect nostalgia, belonging,
Relief, love, coming home,

Touching this, I know the way
And see all around me
Cycles of time and fate
Every now moment ringing
Like a bell, leaving no stain
Upon the mind, only echoes,
      Rippling on water
Every face, each pair of eyes—
The way following the way

Everything where it should be
Nothing misplaced, space
Embraces everything as
A demonstration of the fact
That relationship is what there is
      And all that there is

This feeling is compound,
      And so it will pass
      I know

      But today again,
You have shown me
That life is not a series of moments
With an "Eternal" one waiting somewhere,
Hidden, secret...No, the greatest secret
Is in plain sight, and the greatest power
Of the mind is to forget and create
"Old" from what is always cycling
Back to new, hurling towards resolution
      And back again

Thank you, glorious life, dear home—
May we all discover this place
      We never left

Cosmic Soup

The older I become,
The more life opens
The more I open to life
The more I find myself
      In cosmic soup,
All time and space
Incomprehensible, and
Life a display of
Irresolvable chaos

The older I become,
The less substantial
Everything becomes,
And life reveals itself,
Slowly, as endless
      Patterning
Tornadoes of energy
Spiraling in and around,
Ripping me open to the strange
Fact that there is no solid world
Every crashing wave,
Every rush of wind,
Every smiling face is a vortex,
      An ancestral stream,

The universe waving, and
We are all rivers, flowing
Together and apart,
Mixing and changing,
A million moments
Of life and death, the multiverse
Overlapping without center
      Or circumference

As streams of life, we contain
Ideas, fears, dreams, and
Crashing into one another
We are possessed of each
Others insanities, thinking
Ourselves solid, hoping
Ourselves stable, we panic
And hold onto all the trash
Passing through us, gathering
An island of bad ideas
On which to float and battle
The current pulling us apart

How strange that as we age
We seem to crystallize,
Set more in our ways,
When in every moment
We are falling apart

Birth is the only of cause
      Of death, and
From the moment

We come together, we are
Falling apart, life—the streaming
Container of birth-death

Where do we get this view
      Of solidity?
Humans are strange; the power
Of our ideas—immense
The freedom of choice,
Demonstrated as a world,
Confirmed by hysteria, media,
In the wireless ethers

The older I get, the more
I find myself strange,
Entertained at least
By these strange displays
      Of freedom

Spirit World

Malleable rivers, blood
Streaming digestion, open
Channels, moving together
We are spirit motels, permeable
Bundles of living light, walking
Lunch for the disembodied

Exalting empiricism, we make
The world dead; we make

Ourselves machines; we make
Ourselves idiots, self-enclosed
    In anatomical walls

Bumping about blind, in a vast
World of beings, we trample
The wilderness, scar the earth,
    And shed no tears

    In exile,
Wood, fire, earth, metal, and water
    Circle the globe, swarming,
Lodging in our channels, possessing
The gaps, seeking homes, seeking
Nutrients, nourishment spewed
In all directions by the human buffet

Walking lightly, I bow to fairies & sprites,
Surrounded by rainbow gardens,
    And the world opens
    Into a vision of births,
Millions generated in the warmth of
    Flashing folds

And in this I see the dignity
Of being human and subordinate
To no god, no spirit; I know
Kindness and virtue, and respecting
Everything, I revel in the
Perfect completion of my humanity

Regulating normal, I nourish
Myself, and the ordinary is
Revealed as a phantasm of light
A vast sea of energy and life—
Nothing special needed

Smiling, I know that I do not
Come from god(s); I come from
Parents, who came from parents

Believe it or not, the world
Is alive, and we share this space
With infinite realms, bi-directional
Interrelation and multidimensional
Eating—everything is eating,
And life flows everywhere
In instinctual rhythms, in
Ancestral rivers of reproduction

    Waking up, I see
The world is spirit full of spirits
      My human spirit
      Pointing the Way

Wolf Speaks

    Now,
Wolf speaks
And I renounce, here,
All but humanity

For humanity cries
    With wolf,
From the center of hunger,
    From desire,
From the honesty of fear
    And sleep

Overgrown with process,
That cannot be stopped

What animates us
Cannot be named
    Or known,
Yet we are driven
And in the silence
    Of shame,
Hunger kills; it consumes,
    Everything eats,
And we are forced from within
    By a wisdom
    As natural as sleep
As common as life-death

I do not know mind, and
I cannot find perfection;
I cannot find anything
But compounded things

And everything falls apart
    Under investigation
Everything but hunger,

Springing forth eternal,
Receding into sleep, for

Everything is eating
      And shitting
And the cycle of fear
And desire is all that
Can be trusted

Under blood sky, in brutal cold
Wolf cries, calling forth the truth
      Of desire—that desire
Is the holy fountain of everything
And that in this honesty,
Humanity is free, free to let go
And slide into the empty belly
      Of its own hunger

Free to admit that we are terrified,
Utterly terrified of our own
      Wide open freedom

For this freedom contains
Every nightmare and every dream
And all are free to express—
Nature, in fact, permits everything

      Here,
Wolf speaks, cries out beyond the city
For a return to our natural state—
      For the return to human honesty

Little Deaths

With each beginning,
We must acknowledge,
Always, the tender sadness
Of the slow but steady
      Work of nature

All relationships dancing,
Each person we meet
      In orbit
Around us, the universe
Shimmers, and the source
Of all love and beauty
Radiates, not from the
Eternal, not from any God
But from the dance
Of ordinary life, and
The simple human
      Grief of endings

Big Stupid

Between science and superstition,
      I recommend superstition,
      —less likely to die a ghost

But, between meditation and delusion,
      —better to keep your delusions

At least then you can win sometimes;
Make up things to overcome,
    And overcome them

Best not to meditate—things get revealed
Chaos must be confronted, and
    All progress abandoned

Nothing can be gained from Reality
The spiritual path—a useless pursuit
    For useless people
Enlightenment—foolishness
    To your original nature

Happy are those who read the riddle

Planet of Slums

    Yes,
Our cultures will collapse
This vision we appear to crave,
This planet of slums, a world
Divided, severed from natural rhythm,
    Is manifesting, slowly,
From the collective depth
Of our fears and fantasies
We hover around glowing cubes
And act like insects, swarming,
    Whole cities of ghosts,
    Who look like humans,

Who are, in fact, losing their humanity
In the process of modern life

Many ends will come to pass
Because we want them to,
        Clearly

        In ecstasy,
        We use fuzzy logic
To dream all kinds of confusions,
Nightmares, and justifications,
And, in fevers of assumed
Knowledge, hell bent on survival,
        Armed to the teeth,
With bombs and bad ideas
With gadgets and giz-wigets
        We divide the world
Into perfect reasons to murder
One another and bleed our
        Environment dry

To understand the future,
Look to the present, look
At our actions, clearly
Our structures seek destruction

No problem, the universe
Will provide, for it permits
Everything except an escape
        From our actions

In the dregs of the concrete wild
Urban shamans will dance
Before plastic fire, and we
Will howl at the moon
Through broken windows
And abandoned mini-malls

For beneath the beast
Of modern culture
Beats a trembling heart,
Panic breeding in the mirror
       Of Nature

The two hands of modernity—
God and Mechanism
Creationism and Scientism
Are two insanities,
Foaming at the mouth
In search of security,
In search of answers
In non-conceptual space

Finding nothing in the infinite
Regress of mirrors, we create
Our fate through the ultimate
Freedom of nature, the
Freedom which permits
And embraces everything,
Offering nothing but *karma*
       In response

Of course, our structures will collapse
      All do, in time, no problem
But no rhythm stops; nothing ends
And in the wake of our actions
      We will act again

      And again

Since enlightenment is the source
Of suffering, perhaps, one day
      We will learn—

No structure can survive

Mindful

When what you actually do
      Is revealed—
Congratulations, you have
      Found the Way

Flashing on the Universal

There was a time,
When poets walked
      In gardens, and
The moon reflected its form
In gracious cups of wine

Drinking the spirit down,
Moments flash, and
In a glimpse, everything
Is contained within
And the outside
Is an unknown, stretching
Itself in circles, and I
Burst, turning inwards

Flashing on universality,
The moment folds
And the shame of
Of self-cherishing
Brings with it the
Ancient pattern, this
Daring humanity, this
Loving smallness,
The remembrance
Of precious ignorance

By a River in Assam

Old word stink;
Fresh water flows—
Returning to this Mother
      Land

I smell the stench
      Of heart blossoms
           And Fear

Overwhelmed and lonely
I pry open this heart box
And cast ribbons reckless
    Upon the floor

    Around me are the
Consequences of my humanity
I understand nothing, and
In the echoes of India
Runs the blood between us

Shamanic Blues

Looking down, I see
My hands; here,
    Again...dreaming

The sky opens, *tigles* dance,
And a point of light beside the sun
    Calls me beyond,
Digging my heels, I fly
Into luminosity only to fail,
Flailing my limbs, grasping the sky,
Cursing this dumb body, crashing
Like a rag doll into dirt and trees

Dusting off, I trace my steps to
A threshold where I looked
In the mirror and in an instant
Saw no distinction between

Awake—asleep
Birth—death
Dark—light

Rolling over, I flop off the floor
Back to this human mess—
    This social trance, where
    We rush like mad
    Cramming our hysteria
    Into plastic boxes
Eating numbers, drinking electric light

Asleep—I know I am dreaming
Awake—I know I am dreaming
What is real? Where the hell am I?

In dream—I have seen and felt
A love more pure and genuine
Than anything any person has shown me

In dream—I have felt the presence
Of ancient companions and
In an instant seen the Immortal
Continuity—that I have been dreaming
Since before I was born

    The sun—moon dances;
    Tuesday, again

Stumbling about the human realm
I sit, endless days—legs gathered

Gaze pinned
Relax. Take nothing. Leave nothing.
Be with everything as it is.

I thumb the mala mumbling,
Turning pages of Wisdom Rain

Hearing the Noble Dharma, I weep
With ghosts and demons and know
  I am no different,
Circling forever in displays of Mind

In my dreams, I breathe gnarled smoke
And sit before fire and blood, invoking a
  Ritual of oceans and stars,
Forests and rivers, ancestors
  And animals

Awake—I bumble about in
This technological marvel
Fumbling to make sense
  Of "progress"

"Do something" anxiety
Fills my shoes and I walk
  Into walls,
Opening the wrong doors

  Dreaming,
Whistling the shamanic blues,
I breathe out, and the sun sets,

Again, bringing with it
An ocean of stars, welcoming
        Me to wake up

Crazy Town

Long nosed, red faced,
Bug eyed—mad
        Here, the frantic
Dream, this never enough,
Breeds, and hunger swarms,
Burning the light, flashing forth
        Fantastic death

Tunnel vision, purposeful life
Advantage gained, spinning this:
Particle self; MY pain—special me

Full of plastic, I sit sick, and
My brain squeals wonder—
Where the hell are we going?

The carrot dangles, and
Fire boxes spew us angry
Into social air, earth splinters,
And the fragments fly
Red faces worry—focused, scared
        Time slipping away

Where, I ask, are problems?
>When did we leave?
>Were we ever here?

Spinning in circles, I see,
All around me, fire and metal,
Weapons and brains
Big winners—more losers
Squeezing hypnotic loss
Through iron locks and pain

Seeking happy secrets, I pop and
Spill anxiety all over the floor—
Sorry, I could not hold in
>This flaming shit

Relaxing tension, I giggle
Into naturalness, and goddammit
>My eyes are burning
Wanting out, wanting home,
Wanting return—that's it, let's go

Light bubbles flash in darkness
And a small bird bounces about;
Overflowing my skin, I burst
Into sanity, following the way back
>To useless wonder

Internet

Mass trance, world 'round,
Flickering dreams, here, before
Delusion boxes, scared shitless,
We gather our kidney force and
Hurl vitality into wireless light
Pouring hope into empty symbols,
Savoring remnants of thin humanity

Somewhere, lumbering in darkness,
      Something
            Big
                Feeds

Lost Ghosts

Big world,
Chaos and flow,
Love and hostility,
Heads and hearts,
Fragile and flooded
With bad symbols—
Our fluids dispersed

A million years, of
Ancestral memory,
      Lost ghosts
Seeking love, in angular
      Hope

Looking to leaders, we
Generate a circus
Of poor conduct, and
Countenance is lost
In arrogant hysteria

What is a human being, anyways?

Splitting hairs, we ejaculate
Our sanity into engineering
And loose our appetite
In great white death

     Hurling towards hope,
All around us, ancient symbols
Speak, and our tongues flap nonsense,
Seeking a way back
To the brilliance of
The Great Mother

Filling our blood with anxiety,
Stanford Shamans beat the drum
Of science, erecting death in
Magazines of perpetual embarrassment

     Method without View,
What is the Universe, anyways?

Knowing not where we go,
Where we are, our intelligence

Has run *amok*, possessed
By the swarming dead

World War, Genocide, Slavery,
And Exile—where do you think
They go? These children
  Of modernity

  Our culture is clogged
With a rainbow of the unresolved

Sitting in clouds of pain, I flash
On emptiness and breath in
  Lost children
Taking the pulse, exhaling blue
Light, cultivating countenance,
Liberating my own ghosts
  With open arms

White Clouds

Tracing the tears,
Following footprints,
Sunken in the way
  Of white clouds
Words, immortal symbols,
Speak, and nine lights
Radiate from the Polestar
Fate recorded, opening

The world of Heaven
 Before me

Orphaned

Through Heaven,
I know Earth, and
My cells vibrate, echoing
Ancient songs, and my
Bones whisper sadness,
 Seeking humanity

Born old, I see my tribe
Malnourished, ghosts in
Human form, pale vacuity,
 Exhausted,
 Eating electric air

But perhaps, I am
The ghost, a shadow
Of something long dead
Perhaps we are evolving,
Merging with machines,
And I am the serpent in a
Lunatic trance, beating
A corpse, singing nonsense
 To forgotten stars

Absorbed in trance,
I am an orphan, two hundred

Years a child, without
Parents, wandering
In metallic wilderness

Where do I come from?
I hear stories of the Ancients
And I feel the heartbeat
Of a thousand generations, of
Ancestors honoring the Earth,
      And I weep,
Eating lost fruit
From a plastic mother

Where are the Elders?

Where have our dreams
      Taken us?

Seeking the soil,
Seeking community,
      I howl
And through chords
Of wisdom blood, I
Follow the beating
Heart back to the center
Of Life, back to the summit
Of the great mountain

Choosing humanity, I
Bow to the alter
Of my Ancestors

And know that winter
Always gives way
To sprouting seeds

The Mirror

Twisting, winding
Through the Way; my knots
Unfold, and my channels,
Bidirectional, open into
Flowing Radiance

The circle of Mother and Son
Orbit, filling the cauldron,
And I churn 10,000 ghosts,
My heart bleeding vanity,
Red and White,
Into oceans of Nectar

Filled with tears, I turn
To face the Mirror, and
Echoes of action splinter
Into strange displays

Hosting presence, holding
The Way; everything
That struggles exhausts
Itself, and I am exhausted,
Humbled by the depths
Of Fate and Fortune

Returning to Source,
Losing everything, I sigh
And Immortality is found
In the sweet filaments
      Of Life

Reliance

      Abandon trust!
Nothing is reliable, and
All appearance—dubious
Who said trust was useful?
Everything will let you down

Identifying other, you invoke
Death, and ask to be
      Disappointed

Nothing appears outside
Mind; luminosity—the only
      Teacher

Experience upon experience
Shows nothing but experience

Neither trust nor mistrust
Stay only in your own
      Experience
      Without trust

For no matter what you
Perceive, perception remains
Perfect—a crystal mirror
Hosting infinite reflections
All of which—untrustworthy

Bifurcating, we cannot help
Our broken hearts—always
Disappointed in the dual world
For the day is dark, and all
Teachers fall from grace

Look not to the throne
But only to the left and right
To your fellow human
        Travelers—
Love them completely
And abandon trust, for
The mirror is unconditional
And so is your nature

Prefer neither this nor that
Follow your appetite—trust
Your hunger, for it will reveal
Your immortal nature

Following doing, bubbling
Forward, back to being, I
Open to the *Vajra* Heart
And burn the ties
        Of trust

The Flood

This dearth, concrete,
       Endless, empty;
Where in the flow, in
The crossing of streams,
Will the tomb of Fate
Burst open so fertility
Can go the way of flowers?

The hills, the waters, the
Landscape of my dreams
Flood the sidewalks
Of this dead town, and
       My mind flashes
       On memory too old,
Too beautiful to understand

I dream the Way, and
       My world shrinks
Revealing the unknowable

Hypnotizing—this social
       Trance; I wander
In and out of acceptability,
For my Character is unruly,
And my Humanity suffers
With the Sun and Moon

In the turning of Time
       I am a wild fool,

Stuffing the knotted chord
Into the mouths of merchants

Is there room for humans
In this world of shadows?

Hammering truth, thunder
Rolls from beyond the mind
And the call of liberation
   Waits

Merchant Blues

  Heart—heavy,
In mercantile ways, anxious,
Deal making—this way
   And that

Violent disregarding
   All around

Our nature, I think,
Is too open. Dammit.
Compulsion generating
Unfairness and lack
From universal abundance

Following logic, we must
Admit—our freedom is
The source of all our trouble

Endless choice—a display
    Of natural being

All progress—unproductive
No advantage possible

    Where are we?

Eating concrete, I sigh
As children laugh,
Bringing forward
Eternal cycles and stories
    Of humanity
For we are still human,
And generosity endures

    Habit upon habit,
Enthusiasm and heartache,
Nightmares and dreams—

Nothing can obscure this
Inexhaustible treasury
    Of Space

Amrita

    Too long—restless,
Unbridled—this hot wind
The years have spun wild
Hurling life into death,

45

Water into Fire,
Dispersing heart channels
Into broken vessels,
Empty offerings
Let loose
Into the mouth of sleep,
Hunger feeding the way
Of ghosts

Too long have I been restless,
Following the easy way, old
Water flowing through
Hardened grooves
The past in front of me

After years of wandering,
The royal road home, full
Of weathered footprints, has
Found me, again

At your feet, following
In your footsteps,
Island bells chime, and
I burst into tears, stumbling
Into the pit of this
Charnel ground

Sealing the gates, arriving
Again, finally, at the feet
Of Perfect Masters—the
Wisdom Fire

How many lifetimes
Have I been waiting?
How long have I forgotten?

Surrendering pride, I drink
Nectar from the Immortal
Stream and offer the seed
      Of my very Life
      Into the bellows
      Of the Sun and Moon

Descending in,
—Heart Drops cascade,
And from dark oceans
      Of time and space,
Sapphire love flashes the
Serpent Embrace, and in
An instant, a lifetime of grief
Is shed from this tired body

All around me, visions
Of the primordial dance,
And God smiles at God
Through the mask of strangers
      And pilgrims

Awareness aware; warmth
      Spreads wide
Into the fabric of pristine
      Wakefulness, always
      Present

Presence embracing, always,
The gravity of this polar mass

I spindle open—my corpse
Flayed upon rocks and sky
A mass of channels, a ray in the
      Ocean of Light

For too long has this radiance
Been hidden behind a mask
      Of eloquence, for
Too long has my arrogance
      Sheltered me
      From the round world

      Now,
The real work begins—
Retaining the bridled wind
The electricity within is without
As I unite the Sun and Moon
And ride the Energy of Life
Into the source of space
Where spheres of light,
      The geometry
Of the Great Mother
      Emit trails
Guiding the Way Nowhere

Sound, Light, and Rays

Lost, gone,
Deep—convinced
     Dreaming, I
Release appearances,
And fall freely through
     Nothing
And the wake world
     Sparkles, for
Nothing, it turns out,
Displays everything

The Hammer

     Overflowing,
With vigor, I grasp the keys
And smash at iron locks

     Sick of limitation,
Beyond three times, dark
Water flashes clear,
Reflecting intrinsic light
And all forms become fluid,
Closed symbols bursting
Open into glowing rays

     Everything is hue,
Nothing solid, and in an
Instant, I see my eternality

And know myself as God
And schmuck—
A paradox of loneliness
And perfect contentment,
Following confusion
Into the heart of fullness

One Taste

Seeking a flash,
The promise of essence
Beyond time—I see
Nothing but temporary
Names on a mirror
I cannot see—I know
Of presence but
Can make no object,
And all names turn
To shiny faces, twinkling
Animation of the one taste

Torus

In all honesty,
I think I'm done—
Not sure I can be held
Accountable for continuity,
For controlling fire and air,

For maintaining this bubble
Of ephemeral seriousness

Sorry—I just can't find
        Substance

Nine million lifetimes, and
All I see is dust in light

Wake up! Wake up!

        All senses flow
        From the heart,
And the torus has no center

Seeing through to where
Sight sees back at me, I
Was born to giggle and
Spew rainbow bubbles
From centerless uncertainty

The Ladle

        I cannot believe
I ever took things seriously!
The Sun wheels onward, and
The gate of time flies open,
The great continuity riding
        The scent, bringing
Memories from the birthless mire

51

All I hear is laughter, and the
Saddest story, my greatest pain,
The suffering horror is a wink
In the eye of comedic trance,
The play of a playful nature

Sitting with nothing to stand on
I am the absence of something
Never there to begin with, and
My laughter is dissolution
Folding inward into the play
       Of others

Treasury of Worms

      Death and Sex,
        Beneath fire
And moss, the mind gate
Rots under eternality,
And the streaming pain
       Of Nature,
Of the nature of, impulse,
        Pure and
Permeating within,
This treasury of endlessness
Cycling waste and
Knowledge; gorge the loin;
       Bury me within,
And dig the nails deeper,
For I am sentience driven

Beyond sentimentality
Into fevers of thirst
Writhing in Mind
      Breeding
This treasury of worms

Eating worms, I pin my gaze
And stare death and sex
      Into deathlessness
Burnishing open the space
      Of love

Earth Prayer

O Great Mother—
Here, in the soft glow,
Of yellow autumn light
I spread my heart veins
Into warmth and Sun, gentle,
Through child fingers,
Through Dirt and bone
Into the Ancient Laughter,
The thunder sound of
This Mother-Father Dance

From the base of me, I
Form solid love, and
In humility, I bow
To the Essence, touching

My loin to the grounding
Of our communal hearth

    I—Human!
Prostrate before you and
Your radiant abundance,
For your support flows
Endless honey sweet into
Empty open hearts, filling
Us to the ragged brim
With our own love nature

    In your embrace, I
See the glory of this human pain
Spinning endless, in cycles past,
And I see, too, the story
Of these old human hands,
    Ancient Hands,
The Hands of Day,
The hands that built
The stone walls and
Hunted, planted, gathered,
The grain basket full, the
Bellies 'round the fire,
Under open skies, making love
Before bright red dawns

Here, in the presence
Of you Great Goddess, Earth,
I feel the soul of things insubstantial
And know that I am complete

I feel the great sadness
And appreciate the
Preciousness of birth

Here, before Great Plains,
Between mountains beyond,
In this dense forest Mind,
I pray to you, Essence,
May we never be separated!

For I am dependent upon you!
And I am nourished, always,
By this vast sea of energy welling forth
From the ground inexhaustible

And as I walk upon this earth,
      My feet sink low,
Into mud and root,
And flowers spring
From the festival
Of Life-Death
And in the light of death
I relax into mind-heart balance

—O Great Mother! Free me of this
Poverty with Your reckless Love!

Water Invocation

O Great Father—
Clear Ocean Deep!
Without shore,
Without end, full to
The brim, with life blood
   And sweat

Born from cool blue light
You, the structure, you,
The organizer of this great
   Life principal,
Shimmer on the surface, and
Reflect the Nature
Of all things moving

Here, before crashing waves,
Beneath thundering clouds,
Under rain and sleet,
I weep, and tears break
Steady upon sand and salt

For I—Human!
Embody this Ancient Anger
This misconception,
This Self-Other mistake

And in the wake
Of great ideas
I falter, I stumble

And in the mirror
Of this aggression, and
In thick fog frozen
I—Human, invoke
Your Wisdom, bowing
In humility, to the power
Of oceans and rivers
To the power of water

To this fluid source

Now water, then ice,
One day steam,
Flowing, pumping, raging
Through earth veins,
Carving desert canyons,
Taking form freely,
Wherever you are contained

For you—the great neutrality
Only flow, only reflect,
Only conform, only
To show the essence
Of this Now we create—
Anger, fear, sadness,
Joy, love, freedom
Whatever I create—
This you show me

Here, in cool dawn light,
Floating lazy down

Gentle rivers, peaceful water
Just reflecting sky's tinge
  Here, at water's edge
I peer into the deep unfathomable
And see my own face staring back,
And as the tide settles, as rippling water
Stills, I relax into bright mirror sight

—Great Father! Free me of this
Anger with your ecstatic Wisdom!

Fire Homage

Hail—great Union!
Now, the power descends,
In shadow and sight,
Between us, into the very
Center of this human life,
The erotic fire, the burning love,
The mystic search
For the elusive other

For this universe Is
Itself Desire, desire—our
Greatest power; the tree
Growing around the shade,
  Seeking the sun—
There is desire in this, and

Here in this longing,
My cells yearn to breath,
And I yearn to release
My own nature into light,
Receiving, yielding to Love
Knowing the sting, the fire
Of this direct experience,
The ancient fire of vivid
And intense pain held
Within the chaos of the body,
The chaos of the earth,
Through countless ages
Of wandering the wasteland
Of rebirth, searching in vain
For rest, for security,
And for answers in the
Midst of impermanence,
Emptiness and change

This pain, which we have
Always known, is the pain
Of our longing, the pain
Of our separation
From the spiritual source
It is the ache for a return
To our inherent and
        Divine fullness

For long have we—Humans,
Gathered around fires,
Under open skies,

In ceremony and in ritual,
To share in the naked experience
      Of our humanity

Great Lover, here, around
The fire, we pay our respect
To this terrifying power at
The beginning of all things modern,
Our essence technology,
The womb of war, the
Discriminating birth of
Both terror and love, hope
And fear, the choice before
Us, the power to choose
In the tired hands of this
Ancient Human Condition

Fire, ash, renewal—
Flesh longing faith—
In the wake of the setting sun,
Before the dawn of this old-world darkness
The funeral pyre crumbles, at the feet of this
      Obsidian Sun

—Great Union! Free me of this Longing with your Lusting
Fullness!

Wind Supplication

Great Purposeful Universe!
Life Force Wind!
Clear Emerald Light!
Here, at the center of all things,
In my inmost Self, the eye touches
      The essence,
And the lungs burst open,
Into empty-full, wide open worship,
And we are filled, held from
      Within
With divine intelligence—
Sentient loving will,
Massive Mother Manifest
This action within yourself
To know yourself, with yourself,
      As yourself!

You, Goddess, are the movement
      Of Love-Awareness,
Flowing soft, into all places,
High and low, seeking the
Stagnant death within us,
Bringing renewal to the dark,
      Unsought places,
      Which most abhor,
      Where most fear to feel,
Where Ecstasy dances free this
Shell of limitation, in reckless
Displays of terror and joy,

Pacifying and destroying
This petty fear

Here, in the center of the sky,
You can find me breathing
Filling myself with the courage
To know that All is accomplished

Here, falling through
This vast un-restriction,
      I am content,
To let go of what is beyond
Controlling, and to follow
The flow of this Emerald Breath
      Back to the center
Of the sunlit sky, where
You sound and echo, like laughter,
The call of human freedom
To become full of Life
To speak, to act, to shine
And boom forth your fullness
From the empty depths
Of a Being far beyond me
Like an ancient drum,
      In the open air

I bow and open to You
Life Force Wind!

I smell the fragrance
Of ceremony, and

I hear the call of silver bells
And I am blessed, for
The purpose of life
Is made clear in the wake
Of these endless cycles of action
That all action is the breath of God

—Great Purposeful Universe! Free
Me of this paranoia in your envious embrace!

Space Salutation

Greetings, dear Space!
Great Lord Awareness!
Manifold host beyond,
Loving sexless source

Emerging from the past, here,
        Now, the fetters dance,
And the grip begins
        To unbind

Greetings, dear Light!

The five colors meet,
Between object and eye,
And in finite display,
        I am submerged
In a vast ocean of Heart

Who am I in this world?
    Blown inside open,
    I am wide
And my fear workings
Grasp at nothing blocks

Beyond my pieces,
I am sizeless
Beyond my idols,
I am shapeless

    Gone beyond,
I am dimensionless
In dismembered memory
And between cracks of terror
Springs Love unfathomable

Gone beyond,
    I go
    Where no mind goes

And in the sparkle
    Of your display,
Know I will not

    Return

Morning Mist

The Five Spirits
And the Ancestors
Dance—symbols speak,
Imagination—their playground
My heart is Red Dust,
And the mind is mist
Liberated into space
Knowing nothing of where
I go, everything is a dream,
And all preciousness is lost
In wiggling filaments
Of Light

Mother and Child

Here, at the
Periphery—a drop,
Falling from the crown,
Backward dreaming,
Forward
Harmony, parallel
Vapor, reflecting
Dispersion from the
Center—clear light Heart,
A multiverse of
Empty spheres, full to
The brim with rainbow
Diversity, going out, and out

Where the edge—
The Mother, Clarity, is
Identical to her Child
Within, alternating layers,
Every edge also a Child, the
Beating Heart of another's Center;
Space is clarity, and
Behind the eyes, the Web
Of bodies, space and form, are
Ordinary, nothing there, for
Nothing happens
The spiritual path—a play of
Perception

Darker than Darkness

Threshold—
Unseated, this Dream,
Birth and Death open,
And clarity dawns, the
Great revelation swallowing
Me into centerless space
Flying!

Could it be?

That, ultimately, truth
Is a revelation of Darkness?
This display of light and rays,
Surely, is hosted in an

Immense and vast darkness,
Giving birth to myriad
Structures—all useless,
No knowledge using no
Knowledge to know; this
      Eye—an empty
Hole, filling the darkness
With playful structures
      Of luminosity

Again, and again, this
Dream cannot be maintained
In the Light, and I am
Shattered into referenceless
Wonder—flying everywhere
      In no direction
Fear turns to exhilaration,
      Exclamation, as I
Relax and fall nowhere—
In, out, up, down, left, right
      —All useless

In the Darkness, I hear
The immense inhalation
Of nothing, and, exhaling,
I see the ten thousand
Arise symbolically,
Constructs of flowing
      Light geometry,
Channels made of direction,
Generating reference from

> Desire and Boredom
> Spiralic mandalas of
>   Preciousness
>
> Flying in Space, Darkness
> Reveals turbulent atmosphere,
> And all form is a dance
>   Of internal weather,
> Wind, Fire, and Water condensing
> Into apparent specificity
>
> Relaxing preciousness, the
> Channels merge back into
> An apparent world, and I
> Wake (?); back to this Dream,
> Bumbling, trying, wandering,
> Uncertain of what to do
>   With no knowledge

The Stars know their Way

> Have you any idea,
> Of the ecstasy wrought
> In the colliding
>   Of galaxies?
>
> You are the Earth,
> And the Earth follows
> The Stars; your Essence,
> The twinkling of light

Behind your eyes—
Tadpoles in the Sky,
Vast oceans of wonder,
One taste, flawless;

      You are the open
      Expanse, and your mind is
Deathless, containing all Potential

Let go of preciousness!
And let in the nature
Of everything beyond
      Comparison

The Stars know their Way,
      And so do you,
      For your heart is a Star,
      And the planets orbiting
      Reflect all things orbiting
      For all things orbit;
And the lines of Fate shine

The Land of Sky Blue Wandering

      I have been here
Before, to the edge, of time,
Where rolling clouds pierce
A centerless sky, where
Voices speak gold, and
Coming back, I know the

Story of my immortal
      Heritage from the
Realm of grass and sky

Cutting through fog, the
Dark night gives way to
Memories too old and too
Familiar to be of this life
      A journey long
Tread, opens again, and
Although it is new, I
Am met by strange beings
In a strange realm, who know
      Me, and I them

Dream companions, hidden
Symbols, crack open the sky,
Climbing; in dreams, I
Go up and up and up
To floating worlds beyond

Visions cast circles upon
Circles, and soaring through
Space, I read the language
Of stone, and my fingers
Trace the soft glow
Of tall grass and light
      Golden grain
Echoing the sound of wind

Arriving home, I feel sweet
Currents of love, and hearing
      The call of ancient
      Streams, my heart
      Speaks a truth
Too simple, too close
      To believe

      Rest in wonder

      Always be
amazed—for this is
The Immortal Place,
Where everything is
      New

Vajrabodhi

Spinning, life after life,
How many have I wandered,
Not noticing—this, pure,
Empty cognizance? always
Displaying, always firing,
Everything a dance within,
An expression of, an open
Invitation to recognize
The immaculate space,
      The inexhaustible
      Nature of unborn
Wakefulness; this, the clear

Unidimensional, radial
Expanse, without center,
Finding nothing, seeing
Everything, all inside-out,
Nothing; clear-aware;
Unwavering brightness
Oh, let me fall into rest,
Relax and release into this
Great mother, space—all
Encompassing, the
Simple stage, the playful
      Gaze—let go
Of preciousness, and let your
Mother embrace, for she
Has never wavered, and
      Never will

Raven—Mirror

    Corpse upon corpse,
Circling the mound, flowers
Upon the womb; wolves eat,
And eternal lust descends
      From sky and star
Pecking dead dreams—squawk!
I flap my raven tongue, and out
Falls a Mirror reflecting the Great
      Expanse; crusty lifetimes
Of nonsense crumble, and
The appearance of time and form
Display uncompounded twoness

Riding the wisdom of others
With fearless conduct,
I peek behind the curtain
And tremble before Space
Spiraling in; flowering out
Streaming branches
Of immaculate nothing
Fly into mind rivers like strands
Of pearl and ice, lighting the darkness
Beneath sunbeams and White
All form is the Red Dust of a
Thousand radiant wombs,
Ancestral spectrums of warmth
Drawing us back to birth
Liberating Fate, White and Red unbind,
And this Raven glimpses the Mirror—may
All dreams dissolve into the absolute
Space of unborn, non-arising suchness

Madman

With reckless abandon, I
Let my worldview collapse
And spend this life
In the wonder
Of naked Mind!

Part II
Ritual Fire of the Midnight Sun

2012-2015

GOD IS LIGHT; God is Love; God is the inexorable law of Balance; God is the indivisible, motionless, sexless, non-dimensional, undivided, and unconditioned White Magnetic Light of Omnipotent, Omniscient, and Omnipresent Awareness, the luminous emptiness, the divine darkness, at rest, eternally dividing equilibrium into equal sex-paired opposites through the outpouring of reckless and ecstatic love.

Writers—
(Dedicated to Thomas Merton)

Welcome, Writers—
Here is the water of life
     Dance in it.

Let loose the hidden stop
Of the heart-mind, and
Bring forth an explosion of hope
From your in-most self
Maskless, naked, a living expression
Unified in the flame
Of a purifying honesty

Refuse classification; embrace the ordinary
And defend your innocence,
Rooted in fidelity to life,
Giving freely the gift which remains open
For no man can make the sun rise,
And no woman can make the rain fall

Writers—collective life has divided
One against another
And infected the world
With the deepest metaphysical doubt
We have accepted the price tag
We have used our illusions
To build a commercial world
Of arbitrary values without life or meaning

We have divided, and in this division
We have set one against another
For the purpose of evaluation

Writers—band together in ritual fire,
Denounce the shame,
Denounce the imposture of this poison
And reject classification
Remain outside the insatiable doubt,
Breathe free the unpredictability
And tension toward the New

Do not weave words about life
And expect life to conform,
For there is no magic in words
There is only impermanence,
Unpredictable in all its freedom
There is only life and death
Innocent of manipulation

Be not like those who devour words,
Anxious for tomorrow
Be not a persuader
Obey life and the spirit of life
That calls us to express and revel in the ordinary—
Such is the writer's spirit

Be proud that you are ordinary
Be proud that you are a child of the unknown
Be proud that you are not an expert
And above all, be proud of all the words

Given to us for nothing
For nothing is all we have
And the words point beyond the objects
To a noble, thunderous silence, beyond ideas
Where nothing can be said

Writers—say yes,
For the politician fears us
More than violent revolution
Because we are mad with a therapeutic love
That can change everything

Embrace your madness
Follow your own weird
In your own way

Writers—here is the river,
It never stops moving
And no one can enter this water
Wearing the collective garments
Of public and collective ideas
Feel this water, for beneath your mask
You are naked and simple and honest
And beneath classification,
You are unified and open and free
You are rooted to a love deeper
Than you can imagine
Writers—here,
Here is the water of life,
It is yours
        Dance in it.

In the Land of the Afternoon Light

Knowing not where to start,
I jump headlong into the glimmer,
Headfirst into the radiance of this afternoon light
      Bouncing on the water before me

A dog wanders without a leash
An old man paddles a green canoe,
Stopping briefly to gaze in awe
      At this clear ocean stillness

He floats about the lake's edge,
Gulls sit lazy on the broken down dock,
While beautiful youth chat idly, passing between us,
And the echoes of wind and traffic,
      Fade back into the distance of city streets

Today, I search without a center
For the origin of my tangled web
And in the wind, in the flutter of passing feet
I can feel no solid place
Where I may attach this notion

Of I,
      Of me,
            Of mine,

And still, I feel that nothing will do,
Nothing but this odd act of possession,
Nothing but this long and complicated

Object of desire, constructed from long nights
      Built on the foundations of a false and empty pride

Yet as the radiance of light blooms,
As the air begins to chill,
It dawns on me—that I must give everything up
Especially what I desire most
That here I must bend and give in,
      I must listen to what life tells me

That what I see outside is also within,
And that I am like an empty fist,
      Used to deceive a curious child

And even if I were to cry and curse the past
Even if I were to die, here and now,
The gulls would still sit lazy upon the broken down docks
      Beautiful youth would pass by my
      slumped corpse

And behind me, in the shade of the redwoods
Lovers would still embrace
And send echoes throughout
      The center of a selfless heart

No Roots

Numbness pervades,
And a deep heaviness sinks
From the height of me,

Through the central channel
Of my fireless, hollow body
I am windy, and sting with an icy longing
Too muddy to understand here
And still, I cannot bring myself to feel fully,
For all I want is to cry my bitter tears,
      And feel genuinely
That my tears have no roots,
And that I, too, have no roots,
And that I belong not to this hollow body,
And not to this false feeling within,
Not to this feeling of separation
Of which I walk convinced
That I am incompleteness,
And do not contain the fullness
Of the male and female already within me
O let me dissolve into emptiness,
And arise from nothing, as a deity,
As a colossus, as a body of clear blue light
And fathomless radiant bliss
Let me cry my bitter tears
Let me cry until I am cleansed and gone,
Cleansed of this cruel longing
Let my tears have no roots, so that
Turning inwards, my invocation falls
On deaf ears, and I am left to meet myself
In the dark spaces between the numbing rain
      I am empty; I have no roots

Strangers and Pilgrims

Weathered in time,
Circumstance finite, out of accord,
Knocking about, here,
In the dry air, under the brittle sky,
     The arid expanse
Stretches out wide before me,
And I look forward into the open space
     Of uncertainty,
Anticipating what may come

The years have proven hard,
And, as always, the night awaits
From the moment
The day is set in motion

And around me a bitterness builds,
For this journey, it seems,
Has left me wanting, eternally,
Searching for something I thought lost,
For something made for infinity

Endless days pass between these bars,
Travelers come and go,
And the tavern door swings open,
Bringing forth strangers and pilgrims
From distant deserts
Of loneliness and drought,
The lights above me dim

And reveal a young man, here, fragile
In all his poverty and doubt

What Kind of Human

The flower springs from the footprint,
The first step sunk in the short-long path,
    The daunting unknown,
Decisions made, second guessed, endless
How fear clutters the inner working, and
How our safety binds tight
    The bitter chains

    And yet I know I must go,
        And let go,
Of each breath and of each thought
And of each year I spent searching,
Like so many, for a security inside
    That does not exist

    Haunted by the elusive image
Here, I find, not that security disappears,
But that it never existed at all, and,
Like the island self, as I search
    For a safety within
I find only an impersonal river,
Moving through an impersonal space,
Vacuous, yet somehow full
Of an impersonal love that embraces,

Encloses, and brings us together
Through the destruction of our safety

And so as I sink into this negative space,
And as I look back,
      I obscure everything,
And nowhere am I resolute
For in the mirrors that I erect,
I see myself, and a trail of myself,
Flowing back into what has past
And I cannot help but to ask—
      What kind of human am I?

      What kind of human feels alone?
Only one living out of the universe,
Held fast in the teeth of experience, bound
In his own private universe,
Out of presence, not present,
Stuck in loneliness, crowded by indecision

      And what kind of human will I be?
If here I am broken, and here
I am still fixated, fantasizing, remembering,
      Lost in my own empty promise

For the mirrored past reveals
More than a whimpering form,
It reveals, too, a strength, unbound and

Unharnessed, unsought and unseen,
      And, so, unused and waiting

And this mirror reveals the lion,
Blind and caged by the delusion
Of people peering in, chained to himself
By his own withered strength

For we are blind and hunt and kill for
That which is already within us,
And for that which is already full and waiting,
      That which overflows the chalice
Of the unrecognized heart

And in the dawn, I do see the man,
And more, I see the unrecognized heart
And the fury behind blind eyes,
      Destroying the heart-path

And I see my own desire breeding
With this fury, and my still heart
Roars in the darkness unknown

And this unknown is the heart itself,
For no matter how exalted the mind becomes,
The greatest stranger is, still,
      This one in the heart

And this path, my path, our path,
Must be of the heart
      And we must let go,
We must take care of death now
And cherish the good we make capable,
For in this life, I am only passing through,

And my body is only borrowed,
And this mind is not my own,
For I did not make it—
     The world did
For as the footprints behind me vanish
Like the wake of a ship,
Flowers spring from the cycle of life-death,
And the journey, always beginning,
     Although daunting,
     Is the journey to now let go,
     And let what comes be

Make My Way

It does not make sense, to
Soft eyes looking up from the long dream,
The first, of many, leading into the light
     Of the unfamiliar
The yellow mountains turn over to green,
All roads lead to the center,
And a busyness full of youth
And color and privilege
Opens from odd corners,
Encircled, already, in its own story

I drop my story down into the middle,
Into the ongoing clatter,
And the past, coming together,
Moves about in circles around me,
And none of the loose ends make sense

For the world waded through is murky,
Full of conceptions and ghosts
Projected upon the naked light

To myself, I am a pilgrim,
But to all others,
      I am a stranger,
Projecting my ideas, my ghosts,
Like all the others

Yet the wheels make sense,
      As they turn, and,
Like the leaves, still clinging,
The light rains as I, still breathing,
      Make my way

The Absurd

Welcome to the true theater
      Of the absurd
The very center of this human life,
The erotic fire, the burning love,
      The mystic search
For the elusive other,
The vital need to choose
And be chosen, to cherish
The jewel in the soul
We seek to give freely,
If only to be given in return
      Freely

        The dual flame
Warring eternal between the animal
Nature and the imagination,
The foundations of lust and longing,
The forceful drive of the loin, the breast
That swells and yearns to be held
And cherished above all else
As a one from out the many
A singular element in a storm
Of batting eyes and uncertain choices

I know not how or why
I came to be here,
I can only say that it was me,
I am my own doing, and
I sit heavy at the crossroad,
Paved of my own karmic fault
And by the very life in me,
The subtle sense for which
I yearn to make of this
Odd dance of the sexes,
So far can be nothing
But a cramped futility,
Reaching through iron bars
To a world far outside

My thoughts, my words,
My very bones become
A dry and brittle leaf
Turning in a cruel wind
My breath has escaped me,

And I am weak
In my limbs and in my heart
And although I have walked
The long path 'round the bend
I know nothing of it
And even with an army
Built of the past
Behind me, the confusion,
The game, this brutal stage
On which we bare our inmost
Needs and wants
Is a dense and unforgiving jungle,
And that precious light
Of desire and ambition
To which we adhere and scream,
Is but a splintered web
Of harsh clarity and tangled truth

And after all the occurrence
All the days of action
Taken in unknown directions
In hope towards the end
Of the line drawn in water
Or chiseled in stone,
Taken for it seems unbearable
To sit still and be content alone

And in the heaviest place within,
The place we conceive ourselves,
The idols we build and polish
And place in the heads of others

From before we have even a chance
To learn and let ourselves go
      As we all must do

Sometimes, these visions sing,
Sometimes they dance,
      And sometimes,

      They scream

In desperation, perhaps,
To be something more
Than idols, something more
Than rulers of a universe
Of private experience

Through this mirror,
I see the strangest of all truths
And still I know not
How to reconcile the sway
Held in full over my heart,
For I am nailed to gold,
Chained in iron and platinum
By this play of passion,
The push and pull
Of this out flowing love, and
The dark lamp lit and
Guided through the dark wood
By human need and choice

Yet with my words and mind united,
Together if for even a moment,
I can feel that the peace I seek is here
   Beneath the noise,
Along the dusty road,
Beside the watering fountain,
The sun path lit with sandy footprints,
And voices echoing through
The endless solitary trod
We all traverse, eventually,
In frustration,
   Or, elation

The light turns over
And seeps into the smallest of spaces
Within me, and I am cast open
I am wide and patient
And know this distance
I create will pass in time
And out of me and my life
I become a nerve connected
To the rushing sensation
Of the life pulsing within
The beating wings of a social bird
A comedy for some,
   And a tragic lay for most
Becomes a book, frayed and worn out
By the curious hands
Of an infinite gathering of frustrated youth

Defined in youth
By our unrequited intensity,
        Our lack of reciprocity,
For love cannot be the sole act of one,
Love cannot flow freely
Unless it is received and guided
Lest it flow useless in all directions
Becoming weak and transformed
Into a web of shadows and symbol,
A pale silhouette of love,
An image abused and beaten
In the lost kingdom of social idolatry

Light in the Earth

The tears of a savage sun,
The rays of an awful truth,
Beat down, rough and steady,
On the ground before me,
And out of the earth, born of the earth,
        I come stumbling
Toward conclusions and fantasy

        And my head is empty,
My soul and words, hollow
I am young, and I am lost, and
Like so many of the searchers,
I am banded with the elusive other,
Seeking something elusive, seeking
Some gem buried in the heart

Of the ideal lover, always a mystery,
Gone from the logic of relation,
Always ahead, the beautiful life
So many seek yet so few find

And although I am swimming
In a vast sea of solemn faces and names
In an age full of imagined nobodies
All trying in desperation to be
Something they already are, alive,
With knotted dreams amongst the busy clatter
Of an infinite human mall,
A catalogue of woe and want,
It is obvious and clear,
  I am lost
And cannot feel myself apart
Of any culture masquerading about today
Nor do I feel myself to be part of any tribe,
And all these people before me are distant,
Walking in a realm beyond the senses
An act, a scene of ghosts,
  Vanishing before the start

So, here, before this empty stage,
I sew together a story untrue
  A tale of many lives
Running parallel, for your eyes
So I may understand
A small piece of myself,
So that through this emptiness,
This distance between lives,

I may at least be entertained
And collect my dreams of love
My desires, all of my longings
In this torrential life
Into something that might
      Actually make sense

So at least romance
For me will exist
Even if only for a few fleeting lines
And a companion may
Thrust herself from the deep
And meet me in the open day

This is my call into the wild,
My song being sung
In the hope that it will not
      Go, unheard...

Throne of Confusion

O how the most intelligent,
      And the wisest of us
Can be incapacitated, broken,
Made fools by the subtle grasp
Of love's crushing banter
How quickly this vast, empty awareness
Long sought after,
      Apparently in vain
Can become full, and

Haunted by the ghost of desire
Brought down to walk about, and collide,
With the rest of the miserable youth

To the fellow human hand,
        The hands of the day,
To the lonely ones half asleep,
Walking beside me through this living gate
The torch against the cave wall flickers soft,
And an image of the dual flame comes to life
And brings life with it, burning strong
From both ends of the human wick

Out of the secret garden full
Of the blossoming flower, and the
Petal and stem fallen into slumping form,
Beside the drops of eye water and sweat
From the furrowed brow of the tense men
I sit, between light and illumination,
And the years of the unwelcome
        Become a living mirror
By which to reflect myself
In this awkward stage of understanding

The morning sun fills the yellow earth
From ground to sky, and dancing in the air—
Beam after beam of golden wind,
And here, metallic tables open before half shut eyes,
Revealing an inner city, teaming with old cafes
And pleasantries, bouncing between full hearts,

Acquaintances and old friends,
     Families and disasters

Laughter flutters along the breeze,
And the chatting mass volley their words
Back and forth, attempting the impossible—
     To make each other understand,
To somehow convince and validate themselves
In strings of meaningful sound
Shot like arrows from a needy tongue

And of all the faces I encounter,
     Of all the eyes,
None say a word to me, and not a one
Has an ounce of truth to tell
Of this day and age,
And all lack the fine,
Simple visage of those awake, for
We are all asleep and dreaming, and we are
Still of a time displaced, and
We neither shine nor point our dim lights
Into a singularity—
     We are diffuse and lazy

And the humble among us are replaced
     By armies of miseducated brats,
 Dwelling on into late adulthood
And even our elders are caught looking back!

And as usual I suspect myself,
And cannot help but ask—

When will we be unified?

For the earth and our very selves demand it
And, perhaps, in my own light,
        I create this feeling, for
I, too, am only one among the sleeping brats

Path beyond the Gate

Emerging from the stoned wood,
Following the rubble, along the ivy,
        To the patterns
Growing down from the earthen bricks
The decayed form, once home, now
Broken open, a skeleton upon the dune,
Bones spread, bleached under red and water
Leading the mind along, into the story
From the brilliant crest
To a mass growing between stone
        And filth

I emerged as a child; I gaze back, now,
And in disappointment know
The paradise garden still exists, somewhere

For the tragedy it seems,
Is that I want to live in a different world,
        A different now,
I want to inhabit a world
Where we inhabit the world differently

For the river speaks of it freely,
The mountains dance
Under rolling clouds,
And the patterns exist
Only in the mind's eye
And only in a world
Where there are human minds,
Breathing and sighing, their souls
Waiting just beyond the rusted gate

Persisting in Gray

The week persists in gray,
And I persist in stagnation,
Drifting between cafes and bars
In rhythm with the empty life,
   I observe, and waste time

And the looking glass that leans
Opaque against the mind wall
Unearths, not only the depths
Of myself and solitude,
But the tepid pond of milling feet,
And tornadoes of energy
   Funneling inward

And the light of too many minds
   About to spill over
From their quiet engagements

And to enter unwilling into the public
Arena of nonsensical war

Quiet war
Wars waged between our precious self
Concepts and the little ideas
We cage in the brain span
Of a tense moment,
Struggling to understand direction

The days are long here
In my inactivity the soul becomes dry,
And the canyon of the heart, becomes
Parched and thirsty for experience
And something to fill the boredom void

For what we do in these desperate times
Reflects our character in times of grace and hope,
As both are the magnetic pull of a single truth

And although I am surrounded by life
        And nodding faces,
And the glances point about me,
        I am barred
And there are always walls
Even in an embrace there are walls,
And division, not by choice,
But by design, and if only
We could work our way to the center
Of each other's hidden worlds

Those walls would fall
To the soil of abandoned desires

These are the lonely days
Full of crowded rooms
Full of strangers, caffeine and ink,
Wasted time, and craving
So deep it chips the bone—
These are the days of bardo
The unending days of transition
Into the mystery of adulthood,
The strangest companion

And in all this,
        I observe
And drown myself
        In bitter words

Noisescape

This is the age of noise
And throughout the world
A war is being waged relentless
Against the ground,
Against the pregnant soil
        Of all noise—silence
And the noise has spread it tendrils
Far into the reaches of the inner
And outer life of humanity,
        For I, and not only I,

Am filled with incalculable specters
That haunt my inside halls
The gleaming halls of the mind
Are full of dancing spirits of song
And visions of the past,
Imaginings half created and lost
Before being seen through
To their logical ends

Unable to rest in silence,
  Unable to be still,
    Unable to let the quiet peace
That lies behind all activity
  Shine through,
  I must ask myself—
Do I really seek silence?

Is the peaceful stillness
Of the quiet mind
Really what I desire?
For my actions, my inner drive
  Speaks otherwise
Or, perhaps, I am only
A rider of the rim
On a waterwheel submerged
In a cascading fall,
Left to spin and spin
In the momentum
Of a downward cycle

I, and the rest of my species,
Seem content to drive the spike
Of chaos into the mind cage
Constructed around our society,
And words bursting with hidden agendas
Flood our very dreams,
Our eyes are flashing screens
For advertisements and an entertainment
That must be had, or else,
And although my hunger for silence
And solitude is always there,
Behind the mental seizure
In which we live out our desperation,
In each moment, I seem to run
My thoughts into the ground
In rigid circles and in vain grasping
For something my heart would refuse
   If freely given
So I must ask myself—
What do I truly seek? Is it silence?
If this brain seems only to ride
Along a one way street
And I cannot bring myself just to sit,
Perhaps, it is something else entirely

Emptiness

The emptiness is vast above,
   And also, below,
Permeating and present

In all experience conceivable,
And in all directions, I march,
And find the presence
Of the instanding water
And the virile fire
Of the outstanding spirit,
For both spring from an empty bowl
As sound from silence,
     Light from space,
And every gathering mass
Is full of that vibrating space,
And in the end, how silly it is,
For us, the object of the void,
To take what is empty and fire and change
To be something solid and eternal,
     Solemn and serious,
For although All is great emptiness,
That which perceives is born, and dies,
In the midst of what is, for only a brief moment,
     Solidified

Song on a Gray Oakland Day

Another day on the avenue
The sun warmth behind the receding clouds
Pours in between this concrete canyon, and
This wound split of our quiet city,
This long set stretch of storefronts,
Cafes and watering holes,
     Sits and wanders aimless

Where we pour the blood source of our excess
        Into purple veins

Where we fill our souls and brains
With caffeine and beer,
A resplendent source
For the vodka heart
Where the youth split into strands
        Down a narrow line
Between ghettos and grass

Day and night come and go,
And I breathe with the same life pattern,
The same wave of smiles, the light
That brings in the trashy tide, and
An ebb that flows and peoples up
The empty rooms, bringing life with it
        And language all around
        In an English land
Where language is anything but English,
And the shrinking world becomes an arena
For games where we get the best of one another

Here, on the avenue, where we walk
        In directionless lines
To sit inside music and stare
At the screens we brought along with us,
Where I sit, and hope, as my emotion room
Becomes empty and full again,
To meet another soul like me

Another day on the avenue
Where familiar faces pass me by
In their own worlds, failing to look up

A gray and faded vein
A dream cage built by decades
Of partiality—

Welcome us home
And draw us into your web
For we are empty inside
And full of hunger

The Water of Life

I sit where the song flows,
Where the verse breaks open
Like midnight waves, under the midnight sun,
Where, before a dream,
The light about the wooden floor
Opens this window within
To the plane beyond the whisper,
The hush, to the words of another land,
Far away, telling of truths you could not know,
For they sit differently than your words,
They move in different ways, from different minds,
And it is comforting to know
That the world is not so small,
That in a different day and age
There was adventure, and mystery,

And not the kind that is planned and paid for,
That in another time
Men and women like you loved, and were loved,
And died for that love,
And even when we are faced
With the truth of our own age—
      That we are not here
That we are displaced, misplaced, distracted by screens
Off missing our own stories
To live vicariously through others
      That even now
The song of the doomed is not a sentence,
And that words from another world
Can sing us back to a place where we are free
And can dance like wild fools
      In the water of life

The Pit

How do I feel the essence of life
As if I were trapped
At the bottom of a pit,
Looking up, as if the heavens
Were not laid out above me?

If only I could ascend the walls
Of this pity cell

But how odd the feeling
That although I am far down

In dust and dirt
You are here, with me, equally,
So above, so below,
And that this is only a kind
Of strange madness
That keeps us apart

At the bottom of this vast pit,
The light of the star shines
And illuminates even the most cramped
Of these corners within,
And the heavens trickle down
Like a rainbow waterfall in slow motion

And all that is left is for me to swim upwards
Until my head breaks the clouds,
Pouring the water of god
Onto the dirt below

Bordering on a Dream

Out of the warmth, out of the light,
Life approaches, not from the past,
But from the immediate,
As if poised like a falcon
Before an endless sky,
With only a breath of wind
To guide it on, waiting

The sky has lost its fullness,
As if long ago it shed its tears
In regret, and opened itself vast
Before a cruel desert,
A desert without borders,
A place beyond shadows
Where there is mist
And a shimmering radiance,
Vibrating from the core of things

The very ground is stretched thin,
It pulls the mind in with it

This is the crossroad,
This desert is the life we share,
And it borders a dream,
A dream of the real
That moves beyond the edges
Of this waking life,
Where every being is a projection,
And from my locus,
From the meeting point
Of the physical and the ephemeral,
A crystal string connects
To the rotating spoke
Of a constellation, and a lonely giant
Walks about the floor
        Of creation

This dream surrounds me
Like a cloud moving from darkness to light

And the past, the future,
And desire itself is contained,
And defined in the smallness of words,
The failure of every symbol,
The hand that reaches for All in vain
To the ends of life,
How every action is a cage,
A mask, a mirage,
An attempt to conceal what is formless
      In a fragile form

How all movement is towards perfection,
However slow, however short,
And every grain of sand in this endless desert
Is a cell of the One

And so, I am going nowhere,
      And I arrive,
And my sight is filled with precious reality,
And it is this life itself that is the dream,
And the universe is a dream,
Rotating around an emptiness, expanding,
Running away from the seeking eyes,
The hungry heart that seeks
To imprison truth only for itself,
And I return to the warmth
From which I am born
In every instant,
With every thought,
Dreaming within a dream,
Dying under a desert sun,

Bordering an ocean of endless waves,
Surrounded my mist and cloud,
Moving from darkness to light

A Private Sadness

Here, sunken beneath the morning,
Reading of an Ancient Rain,
The dream of four thousand lonely nights
Has spread its rotting fingers
Into the mind's eye,
And the swelling vision
Of twenty generations
Has flopped its battered carcass
Onto the shores of a stony stream,
A black stream beneath the streets,
Where monsters crawl over bones
And cobblestone slabs,
And water drips in rhythm
With the footsteps above

My country is pregnant,
Filling day after day with voices crying out,
Only to be subverted low into a digital feed,
Drowned by the well by a weeping hand
That clatters on bloody keys,
And the dry sun spreads slow and yellow
Across the arid land,
Connecting a myriad of cities, I do not know
To the stark fact that I do not know my own,

And cannot, for we, all of us,
Contain a universe of private sadness
And our triumphs remain quiet
As the world we share
Marches on in confusion

Psychic Sexual Fury

The trees slant, the sky runs,
Forms move about
  In pairs and patterns,
And a persistent confusion
  Reveals the pulse
That burns from within
And sets me on fire, from the inside, out
At the very sight, the flash of feminine fullness,
  Swaying and trembling,
Suggesting slightly beneath a veiled form,
  Suggesting the weakness
Of my starving heart and brain
The energy of explosion, of radiation,
  That flows in rivers and drops
Throughout my circulating orbit,
Yearning to burst, dying for release,
Freedom from the failures and fixations,
  The breaking of the dam
So the rest of me can relax

Somehow

That this mind, pervading within,
Is felt, thick and opaque,
And somehow full of a tangible form
Undefined, yet moving
Like a tangled web surrounding an infinite space
Full of light, projecting a myriad of pattern
Through a dense gathering
Of its own knotted arms

And somehow, I am at the center of all this,
Moving through the world
Discerning, somehow, a vague
And wayward path, defined in ways
I can feel, yet cannot explain,
And somehow, I know myself as a series of shadows
Against a wall scarred with the remnants
      Of teeth and nails

Somehow, I am awake
And asleep at the same time
And act as a projection of the most unconscious
Lusts and desires with my feet somehow rooted
In universal presence
A still center orbited by rock and fire and ice

And somehow, I am always driven to transcend
And cancel myself out, all at once,
      The plus and the minus charge,
To flash into mist and emptiness

In a violent blink of impressions,
And somehow, leave with it a source
Of pervading love and service

If only, somehow, I could become extinct inside
And be like a wandering eye that creates
Neither sound nor movement,
Neither concept nor thought,
And so live, somehow,
As an eternal well of death,
Spewing forth an ever-renewing life

And be, somehow, the clear light that is
Beyond all opposites, yet still, somehow, within

Old City

Old city, life stirring the dirt streets,
The faint scent of plastic and urine

Old city, not so old,
        For after all,

The sun burns again for the city
Between the ocean and shadow
Where new life springs from a communal soil,
Beneath the concrete, beneath husk and feet
Scurrying about the after-morning glow

Old city, not so old,
　　　After all

Where the beat died long ago
Only to be replaced with an array of homeless minds
Lost, long ago, in the mystic world
Of a non-mystic time, out of time,
Where all run to dream ourselves different
In crowds of lonely space

Old city, not so old,
　　　For after all,

We are born between the echoes of others
And out of sound, out of light,
A city is made solid and tired
With the patter of endless feet
Who dream, after all, of old city scenes
And an old world pain

Untitled

The young women are confused
About their youth
　　　And the strong men
Have no strength to see themselves

　　　The stars are starless

No light for the dark days of youth

And the women are facing backwards
In the forgotten fantasies
Of young men who fancy themselves
      Old and wise

The Strange Sadness is Free

Cut off from a world
That lives and dies in memory,
A place I know is somehow right here,
Yet distant, fleeting and still,
And like all things—my own creation
      Is it real?
A shadow of the mind,
A doorway back to my youth
When I was, somehow, more here,
Embedded in a vibratory field
Permeating everything,
A vision of myself, small and fragile
A smiling face, a pile of autumn leaves
      And white blond hair
Toys strewn about a stranger's home
Where the magic filled the hours and air
Where every garden, every grove
Was the sacred land of fairies
Who nurtured me in their cotton arms
And brought me back to a life behind time
When sanity meant believing

In what could not be seen,
The roots were my feet,
The branches my arms,
The leaves and petals my fingers and hair,
And I could die without sadness
And emerge from the stony wood
As a belt of mist with fiery veins
And a thorny tongue,
Enchanted smell, the sound of the flute,
Words of another world,
Show yourself in this concrete tomb,
Bring me the treasure of the prince's tears,
Show me the games the angels play,
And walk with me along the lights edge
Between a dream and a living truth,
Wrap my mind in your diamond net
And pull me into the real,
       Out of this madness,
Out of this isolated cell,
Back to the magic land of not-me,
Where I am free to be the ocean,
Free to be a cloud present in night and day
Free to bury my memories in the damp soil
And run naked in the shame and silence

Awful Man

Surely, I am an awful man,
For I do not know myself
I am the pain of other men's words,

The dark night of the dreaming dead,
The poet of an ancient sadness
Sitting here I am beaten on all sides
By my own tragic contradictions,
Thrashing against the walls of my heart,
Searching for the secret lock,
Fumbling with an eternally changing key
The cold rain of the solitary love
Torn to bits by the crying lions, so
That I may know the iron passage
From my heart-gate to this open field
And revel in the dawning of the harvest moon,
The push and pull of the forever dance,
The fire fist, the earth writhing
Beneath a conquering beast
Monstrous and free to be tamed, or not,
For I have seen the oxen tracks
      And tamed a baby deer on accident,
Laughing as the source spreads its mirth
Into the market of an infinite karma

Surely, I am an awful man,
For I am both honest and deceived
I let my heart and feelings run wild
      In a foreign land,
And I shrink in terror as I am ridden
By a demon of the ancient sadness

And it is worse that I am two,
And I writhe in my twoness
As my mind and body form separate spheres

In empty space
For, surely, I am an awful man
Who moves about, blind, directionless,
Searching for the way in,
A way back, searching for
A way out of this ancient sadness

Not Two

Known, now, to have always been
The two halves I contain
        One called life
            Another called death
Enlightenment happens infinity
And I am born always
From the folds of an impermanent god

I am night,
        And I am also day

I swell with the expanding dream
And recede with the devil into zero,
        I am zero

The wind that moves with us
The now and the nothing
The two halves of truth
        Always, will be,
Not a thing, but a doing, always done

Abiding in Confusion

Abiding in confusion,
Down the blind alleys
Of the long-followed reflections
The more I indulge in investigation,
The greater the confusion swells
And becomes full of narrowness
   And indecision
The mind's eye flickers about in this vast web,
Following the light, dancing
From one surface to the next,
   And, where am I?
   Deep in the mire of doubt,
   Deep within a falsehood,
   Deep in the center of an iron ball,
Rolling in dissatisfaction
Through fields of distraction and misery
   What do you want?
I ask myself
And I do not have a clue—
   Let be, let be
Echoes the past
Complete the confusion, and
Pay no mind to discernment and desire,
For it seems the distance between eyes and union
Is too much for this fool
To make sense of here
   Abiding in confusion
I am like a blind man in an ocean of light
Listening patiently

For the sound of clarity
To arise from the deep

Mandala

      Contemplating,
The clear expanse of this blue infinity
Now, as this *mandala* turns,
      As this world turns,
The male spills over into the female,
And I can see the pure spacious mind
As it has always been
Free from dust, free of pollution
Like the sky, like space itself
And every toxic cloud I excrete
Into the deep blue of the expanding heart
Dissolves, arises and passes away
Insubstantial, solid as a gathering of atoms,
And in this space my path becomes clear,
It is in the union of energy and space
Within me that I complete the male-female dance,
Not without, but within, the eternal embrace
Already full,
      Already there,
          Already me

Untitled

Repetition and rhythm,
    Back to the forward force
The rhythms of the deep spacious mind
    The rhythms of the beyond beneath
Where the beneath is beyond, and the
    Behind behind, and the heart is
    bound here
In the rhythm between the in-between,
    The outside space, and
The pulsing is within the in the
    Out, in, out, in and out
Of the outbound breath
    Repetition and rhythm,
Deep in the depths
    Of the spacious mind,
Spaced out and centered
    In the center of the source,
Nearer and near to the nearest
    Truth

Breaking Through; Crossing Over

The sign rings,
The piercing thought,
The clarity that creates,
    The image formed
The dream that divides
Bathed in the fiery answer,

Born from within,
Born from the light
Out of the luminosity,
Dreaming myself awake

Shattered by the pain, familiar in
The sight fixated in the reflection,
The lapse of the judgment, false,
Collapsing, now, before me,
   Before this, before us
The words fail, the embrace weakens
Lost in the darkness of the dream

Lend to me your confident answer
For mine collapses, in you,
Gone in the stare of the golden face,
The poison beneath the eye dissolves
The cycle crests, rising and falling,
   Released

And in the space between the words
The clarity comes, too late, and always
The image before the altar of the ideal
   Collapses
In the hands of our pleasure and grasping
And again, we are here, together
Naked at arm's length

And the sign rings clear,
Cutting through the fog of the familiar
And I am lost, mistaken

In this emptiness I thought was me,
And the long road,
    The knot eternal,
        The path plumbing the deep,
The lead weight of awareness,
The joke of the certain fails
    And all fails
To maintain the consistent fact
And all becomes, in an instant, old,
Dust and paradox, dreaming again
In the dark night, an
Insight into the sleeping fear

Lend me, please,
Your certainty in yourself,
For mine wanes with the coming
Of the ancient rain,
And here, the forest surrounds me, and
The wilderness comes from within,
    Projected throughout,
And above all else,
    I am wrong; I am mistaken
And I am worth only
What I am told, by you,
Measured against the heart
Within the burden, guided
By the hands of the other

Empty Eye

The eye approaches,
　　　The object rests,
And, in itself, believes
The full and inherent real

And the body is labeled
　　　As this or that, and,
Unknowingly, I approach life
With nothing but my odd labels,
And my restless eye,
　　　Discerning this and that
Dividing, conquering,
Dissecting the ephemeral
Convincing myself correct

And so, as usual, I struggle,
Fighting for the security,
　　　Fighting to maintain my labels
Fixed upon the bursting form
Of an impermanent fire
And, breaking apart, I search,
And search, and find nothing

I pull apart the seems
　　　Of this skin
And cannot find a "thing"
I pull myself apart, and find
I am only empty within

And, yet, still I am breathing,
Still the rhythm persists,
And still I can look,
Still the eye approaches the object,
      As uncertainty prevails

And, as I make things real,
So, I am dreaming

And so, I expose my lunacy
To my own fevered questions,
And I know we are all collections,
      Galleries,
Empty airy nothings, and I know
That I am a mass of bubbles
Arising and passing away to where
      We do not know

And how solid it all appears!
How real we make the stories of the mind
How readily our labels
Fail our own investigations

And in each moment, I reify this name,
And clench my emptiness upon itself,
Projecting the strangeness
      Into a future as solid
          As the space which allows it

And although I know the eye is empty,
I feel it full, I feel it inherent,

Existing like the grain in the wood,
The fiber in the muscle, spontaneous,
          Of itself so

And this restless eye scans and schemes
And wants, and craves, and wishes on
          For it wants to stay asleep and dreaming,
It wants, it seems, to win, it wants
Only to be successful in this waking dream,
          For the eye which sees
                    Cannot see itself
The sword that cuts
          Cannot cut itself,
The fire burning
          Cannot burn itself,
                    And the water
Cannot become wet

Nothing cannot be something,
For the emptiness, too, is empty
And my greatest tragedy is, only,
A label upon a collection
          Of rainbow light

Progenitor

How endless we turn the wheel
And bind deep the blood
Running within us,
Out of this past,

Out of the story,
      Here we bow,
And, in blind credulity, seek,
For ourselves, as ourselves,
The oldest of human darkness

For here we are always together,
And here, in this breathing dark,
      We gather, hand in hand,
To wreathe our pain around the light,
And open our veins to the coming day

And now, together,
We must face this day
And all that we have brought to it,
We must crawl through this valley
      Of thorns and bile,
And drink deep the poison we create

For we drown in our poisons,
And we run, in haste,
      From darkness to darkness
For as long as we fail the origin,
And for as long as we remain centered
In this small, impermanent, empty self

And I will always help you,
For together we are alone,
Together we are abandoned,
      Not by any person,

But by our own culture, and by a system
That drowns, like us, in its own poison

     And yes,
I will always help you,
For the longer I walk a narrow path
Through this strange world,
The more I know that this world
               —is a drama,
And that in truth, we can only witness,

And how dramatic it all is,
How odd the comedies we create,
Full of both night and day, so odd
How we turn the wheel in the dark,
Seeking the light with crippled hands
         And with closed eyes, and

     Now, here,
We are at the end of a long road,
We have wound tight the wheel,
And it has unwound

We have spun the wheel with our actions,
And no outside force
Has made us unhappy,
We have done everything to ourselves,
For the origin is within,
And the without is within,
And the time has come
To accept our own shadows,

For our demons are seen only
In mirrors, and nothing is beyond
Our power to transcend

And here, in this crowded valley,
The blood runs upon the red earth,
And the figure lurking in the shadow
    —is you

In darkness, you drank deep the poison,
Knowing that this poison is the creation of mind,
    And the mind alone

So, gather and hold gentle
The hands in the dark,
For they are not strangers,
They belong to beings like you,
And no matter the how and the why,
    Know they seek the same happiness,
They seek only to return to their origin,
To their original nature

So, hold your fellow human hands,
And, in recognition and responsibility,
Let the poison consume,
And in our center space,
Let us burn this wheel to the ground,
So it may dispel the darkness around us,
For without the dark and the light,
No shadows exist,
And it is in this wisdom alone

That we can walk
From darkness to light

Metanoia

The I divided sits in the shadow
Witnessing the fall,
The fearful distance spreading within,
    Grows in its distance

The gadgets click endless around us,
Growing in their luminosity,
Lighting faces in the dark,
Lighting the space in this growing distance

And the speed of this age increases,
The gravity of the future tugs
At the fingers and at the eyes,
And the mind clicks frantic
In rhythmic steps along with it

Thoughts grow from garbage
In this negative, fertile distance,
And the I divided ponders
With a terrifying imagination

And the speed sinks inside,
Driving the fixation into the veins
Of a divided family,
For in this division lies the seed

Of an immense heaven-hell,
And here our illusions breed

But the self, small, sits too
In the shadow of the eternal breath,
And around it circle planets and suns,
Flaring into emptiness and space,
And the rhythm of galaxies
       Is musical time

       Here thought stops
And the distance breeds awe and wonder,
And, for an instant, brings together
The far ends of a single magnet

For a moment there is zero,
And the plus minus cancel,
Revealing the echo of the source,
And the echo is all that can be seen,
And in a flash, impermanence polarizes,
Fermenting all matter into existence
For between the separation of lightning
Sits the self divided,
Now alone, small inside, breathing
An immense and fearful distance

And again, the gadgets whirl and click
And flash all around us,
And again, the speed spins the world fast
On a magnetic axis,
And, for at least this moment,

The little ones crawl
From special zero to fear,
And our future potential
Remains a cold metal tomb,
Born from an alien distance

The Stoned Wood

The canyon opens the earth,
Following the sun, bewildered,
The rays peer through crystal
Deep into the glade,
     Behind the eyes,
The love revolves,
And the current of the nerve
Flows back to the place of origin
Where the individual is the universe
And the moment, eternity

The Forest of the Faded Wisdom

The waning of tradition,
The burning layers divine,
The forest of the faded wisdom,
The sun behind the darkness
     Of the intimate wild,
Standing in the far shadow,
Near birds and water,

Where the city unfolds
    In silence, in distance,
Under a falling snow,
Where the tired voices speak, muffled
Behind the closing of windows, in openings
Where the old mind sleeps,
Dreaming of what it does not know,
Longing for the return to openness,
    To the space within

Long have we done this,
Long have we gathered around fires
To let loose the stone gates
Around the beating of our hearts
To meet the truth naked, and
    In trust

For too long we have beat our wings
Under the cold sky,
And called to the ancient stillness
    Within the fire
So that we may feel,
So that we may touch and hold close
The fullness of our pain and love,
Only to find, now,
The dullness of severed roots
And the numbness of a body abused,
In place of ecstatic rivers,
Flowing in continual rhythm, always,
    Back to the origin of our inner fire

And as the water of sensation flows on,
Beneath ice and dirt and wood,
I stand at the call of the forest
Speechless and still, staring
Into the face of the forgotten body,
Seeing it in the eyes of children
Hearing of what the sorrow tells,
Beneath the voice, beneath
The endless call of the human end,
  The wild cry for the fathom long return
Back to the darkness of the body,
Back to the mystery of the forest, of the earth
Calling now, as always, with longing
Into the cavernous deep, into
The thunderous echoes
  Of fire and rain

Our wisdom has long faded,
And we can neither feel nor sense,
For we walk about this earth,
Thinking ourselves alone and separate and lost
Standing, now, not in the forest,
  But in the brutal city
For as long as we worship the growing distance,
That distance defines us, and the fire
Of our innate wisdom fades

Torch of Uncertainty

The terrifying wail,
The fear of the wide-open expanse,
The space pervading,
How strange that each moment
        Is unprecedented,
For at the same time,
The cage seems to bind tight,
And the endless loop of the mind,
        On a singular journey,
Seems to hold fast, waiting,
As if to find, somehow, a home
Between the flashing of screens
And the bright promise
Of technological story

The dream of more,
The passing of days
        Behind fog and mirror
The not sureness–
How does one live?
        Really?

In the end, with so much wisdom given,
And so many words received,
Still the flatness persists, empty,
Subtle, beneath discernment and judgment,
As if somehow, we have lived in utter fear,
On the verge of great discovery, unwilling,
Sitting on the edge of a vast penetrating abyss,

For years, and, knowing it, waiting
With the same lunatic hope
      Held throughout history,
For the fruition of an impossibility

For together we dance and pray,
Together we don the me-mask
And confuse each other with wrong ideas
As if, someday, they will work

I have heard the stories of the fearless
I have read the wisdom of millennia
I have heard the past speak,
Through silver and blood,
And, walking the narrow path of culture,
I have seen the harrowing of modern death,
      The end of the line,
I have stood where an atomic bomb fell
And known death and life together,
      In the same breath, in the same heartbeat

For the heart that beats in this body,
Is the same heart that beat, long ago,
      In the un-harvest grain,
Among people who did not think the grass
And buffalo so different than we,
And, equally, this heart beats now,
In wall-street men and murderers,
For the expanse of our being contains both
And supports the ground of all humanity equally
      In a terrifying openness

For as long as it remains "other,"
The divinity of space
Will prevent no such catastrophe
For it cares for nothing of the pain
We must pass through
In order to grow
And life has no good reason to transform us
      Why should it?
We may spend our days stuck
In endless loops, and we may very well
Spend an eternity uncertain, and
We may turn this planet into a sun,
Forged by our atomic fire
If we cannot answer this question
About how to live in our own groundless center
Of complete and utter openness

For we were born falling
      Through empty space,
Clinging to the rock of ages,
And we have thus far succeeded
In ignoring the terrifying wail
Of the saints and sages immemorial,
Who came only to tell us
Of our original nature,
Of our fundamental sanity—
That we are the spark,
The warm fire at the earth point of infinity,
The center everywhere and nowhere,
And that the only answer left to us
      Is complete fearlessness

For we have asked for,
And we have been given enough words—
It is now time to live them

Mountain

Of years walking this path,
And hearing the echoes
      Of primordial sound,
Seeing the sun shadow cast
From behind distant land

From the canyon of shame and fear,
Past the volcanoes of pride,
Weary, beyond the doubtful desert,
Life and limb lost in the jungles of confusion,
Now before the ascent of the great mountain,
The pilgrim turns, and in the shadow,
Knows the presence of beasts and angels,
And the wild scent of flowers
      Just around the bend

And in this shadow,
Confusion dawns as the wisdom
      Of clear seeing,
And self-knowledge comes
At the price of our falling apart

For the long path leads, in time, with hope,
To the vision of our spiritual greed,

And to the knowing
Of our deepest motivation—
    To save ourselves, and,
Through even the most profound of disciplines,
Perpetuate the precious story,
And the feeling of separation and self, and
To know that one of two things must die,

For the ascent of the mountain,
    The ascent to truth,
Leads one deep into the space of the all and nothing,
And a story can no more make this climb
    Than a judgment can

Soma

The furthering decent,
The somatic center felt,
The smallness of life, burst open,
    And I am revealed,
As a universe in myself
A universe of cells
Each cell a universe also,
And each a center,
Of experience,
    Of awareness,
        Of emotion,
    Of intelligence,
And through this net
    Of universe,

I know that I, too, am only a cell
Embedded in the great body
In the awareness that continues
To expand and contract,
Reflecting, always,
The transparent truth—
That universe within universe, is,
In one turn, empty, and
The clear light behind appearances,
        Shines through

The Cosmic Clock

The secret of light,
The secret of humanity,
The Silent Voice, whispering always,
In the deep place
Of consciousness, with
Every desire written upon the heart,
Returning to the still point
        Of the One light

In the wave lies the secret
        Of creation,
And in the nature of light,
        Unfolding and refolding,
The pendulum swings,
Between life and death, between
        Growth and decay
Life, as one, constituting life-death

And all matter is electric,
Electricity, the tension between
      Rest and action,
And humanity, as we are,
Progressing in cycles,
Remain dynamically unaware
      Of the souls and seeds of things
For behind the scenes
Of this cosmic cinema
      Of light illusion,
Ticks the rhythmic balanced interchange
Of the cosmic clock

You, too, go out into the Desert

I am human! And
I weep inside, for I am ruled by the fear
Of facing poverty and void

In this festival of rain
      I feel alien,
For this rain brings no renewal to the city
But only life to our perpetual fear,
Highlighting a rhythm no clock can measure,
A rhythm which does not conform
To the inane rules of thought

I weep inside because I am estranged,
And the deep corners of my mind sleep
Between the flashings of dead mechanism,

Lulled into security by the hum of machinery
That does not sleep

    In sleep,
I dream of confusion and sound,
And I fear the rain
    Because I do not know its intimacy
I carry the burden of illusion
    Because I cannot bear to lay it down,
I have spent my life in the safety of the social womb,
Guarding my nakedness
From the chaos in water and sun,
From the pain of growth and decay

I have not been emancipated from artificial need,
And rather than surrender to the rain,
Rather that I should shed this fabricated skin,
I instead fold my pain
Between the warmth of impersonal screens,
    Between story and word,
Enclosed in the womb of myth and prejudice

In this desert of loneliness,
I have not yet found myself alone,
For every time I am born again,
In the song of the present,
I hide from the immensity of rain
And from the uselessness of flowers and mud,
From what lies beyond the myth of the city

Facing death and nothingness,
In each boom, from behind the deep mountain ridge,
In each confrontation with the absence,
      I turn to fear
And approximate god with a shadow
Born from a need that cannot be fulfilled

I am alien to the noise of cities,
And yet I weep and cradle an electric being,
And in my heart, I hear the call of the forest,
For an advance into desert solitude,
Where there is neither center nor circumference,
Where emptiness is sanity,
So that I can assume the anguish
And the inescapable condition
      Of self-cherishing,
The condition of the modern person,
In what has become a society of monsters,
      Incredible and hideous,
Where solitude has become absurd,
And the low places are filled slowly
By the myth that the city alone is real

I am tired of the arrogance,
Tired of the approximation that covers
The sensitivity of skin and naked flesh

I weep, for I am human!
      Let me scream,
Let me face this poverty
And renounce empirical self

So that I may love everyone equally
　　　Let me exist silently,
Liberated from the life of the useful

Revelations

Here, beside clear waters,
　　　A burning wilderness
Down, through the soft light,
　　　Total poverty
Back, beyond receding shores,
　　　A waste inexhaustible
Here, content to be lost,
I turn endless, through thoughts,
Searching for a way back to nowhere,
Only to know, that despite the poverty,
Despite the cycle of pain and time—
Poverty precedes and hosts everything
And that there, behind the light—
　　　Love, and
Beneath the space—awareness

Ein Sof

Edges relax,
And the mind corners dissolve
　　　Into boundlessness

Open words, open wounds, open heart,
  Blown open

Sinking into Earth space, now,
In the belly of paradox, manifold,
Moving beyond shadow and structure,
Auguring down into vertical dimensionality,
  The horizontal transparent

Beyond boundaries,
I fly into wide open nothing
And cannot find an end to things,
Incomplete and insubstantial,
  Void and empty

The pettiness of a limitation,
  Soft and supple,
A malleable form filling the open body,
  Mind encompasses,
And without end is this diamond heart

Filled with beings,
I sense my arms and legs, the belly center,
And the sun burns through cloud
  And mountain green

The world is crystalline structure
The mind splinters and returns,
To soften, shimmering and still

The more I look,
The more boarders elude me
But it does not matter
To another body
In the crowded mass

Soul Ship

Emerging,
Soul is revealed, at last

For too long, I searched for you
As an object, finally,
To know you through being,
To see without looking,
This organ of experience

For I am my experience
And can be nothing else

For too long, I have felt
The cold numb hands
Of spiritual death,
The world reduced to projection,
As if removed from origin
By an accent
Into the dead madness
Of the mind,
And into a violent constriction
Of the body

Too long, have I slept
    In this cocoon,
    Looking inwards

But it had to be done,
For when have I been less by dying?
How can I ascend without oscillation?
The secret of creation lies in the wave,
    And no process ends,
For appearance is explained
Not through the particulate,
    But through emission,
Through the vacillation of lovers
In eternal embrace,
All embrace made possible, only,
By the emptiness of homogeneous
Fields and dimensionality

Knowledge has dropped
    Into the fundamental,
Into the unity of the apparent other,
Body and mind are contained
In vibrancy, in brightness, resting
In the grove of expanding fields
    And conscious presence

    The lines blur,
And what was outside is now
A palpable matrix of qualities
    Beyond fixation, not two,
And life itself is felt

And sensed through inner senses
Flipped inside out, into new worlds
Of surprise and wonder,
Where I am born in each step

Out of beginningless time, without end,
This drop soul emerged, contained
As an impressionable entity, in the ocean,
      At the whim of an ongoing flow,
Made helpless by the abundance of choice,
And through endless cycles,
      Spiraling outwards,
The point of existence was touched,
      At last,
In the body, as the body,
And the inner journey home began,
As the decent into the fundamental
      Pulling aside the veils
To reveal the presence
Of a larger contextual awareness
And the luminous sight of experience
      Behind empty eyes
      And cascading nerves

Finally, you are revealed,
As sensitivity, as the relaxing of form,
As the dance of perfect divinity

And the dance reveals the stage,
And the stage reveals the structure,
And the depth of inquiry

Runs to escape the investigation
Of the infinite display, the pulse,
Of essence

October Sight

The light surrounds me,
And between the enormity
Of sky and tree,
The leaves float
Yellow autumn down

O Goddess,
You are the letting go,
The space shining
Between the mind grasp,
Where longing bursts open
Into freedom sight,
And the gentle way
Is found flowing

Not beyond pain but through it
Through the shadow
Of this adolescence,
For the world suffers,
And the way out
Is the way in

The light is the way in

Silence Unbroken

Here—the Silent field.
　　　It goes out unbounded,
　　　Into great distance,
From withoutside within,
And out beyond again

Space and Energy,
Flow upward, welling forth
This fountain of dreams

Like a memory long faded
I am concealed
I, silence, unmoving
Fill eternal night

And from me,
The fractal turns inward,
　　　Forgetting

Stray Birds and Sunbeams on the Island City of Anywhere

I
It forever moves.

II

The sun behind a distant mountain sings of a deep longing, the escape to places beyond bone and thirst.

III

This is a creating universe, not a created one, composed of moving light waves which spring from a calm sea of the one still light.

IV

I want to live magnificently without fear of making mistakes.

V

We spend lifetimes imagining the divine distant, inaccessible, and invisible, while steeped in her burning layers; in a world completely transparent, the light of the uncreated shines through.

VI

There is no power in thinking, but only in knowing motion from stillness.

VII

All unity is static, all separation dynamic.

VIII

Water cannot be drawn from an empty well, nor can clear water be drawn from a muddied one.

IX

No idea of the mind can become matter.

X

All of the six senses are but the one sense of feeling.

XI

Humanity has, practically, no knowledge and but the slightest suspicion of its spiritual inheritance.

XII

Sensation is the electrical awareness of wave motion from other waves.

XIII

Faster than the wind, the mind believes.

XIV

We, actors of the play, emerge still, barely, from the dark of our jungle; thinking has just begun to surpass sensation.

XV

Utilize what you are; leave no part of your being unfilled with being.

XVI

It is the rattling of my own voice that grows loud, and, hearing the cries of war, I am ashamed to be human.

XVII

The glow of city lights flicker, spattering the unseen shore of silent streets, where the homeless slum in certain rapture.

XVIII

Luminosity fills the world, and I cannot tell if her brightness is inside or out.

XIX

Ideas and wisdoms flutter through me like a rustling of leaves; they have their time and become nothing but memories.

XX

The feeling that I exist at all is perpetual surprise; in rest I am action.

XXI

On the fringe of city streets, the wind howls, unaware of human confusion.

XXII

The heart finds her song when she finds her freedom.

XXIII

I cannot see my incompleteness, for it is the incompleteness that is looking.

XXIV

Life is motion.

XXV

We meet with nothing to say, and for this I have been long waiting.

XXVI

Longing is for what is sensed but never felt, felt but never seen, seen but never known, known but never lived.

XXVII

Imagining the eternal, I feel the freedom of passing away.

XXVIII

The Earth wells up through my bubbling feet, and my belly is nourished by my demons.

XXIX

Those who believe in God are deemed incurable; God is not to believed, explained, or discussed; God is only to be lived.

XXX

Do not stop to gather your thoughts—move on, for your thoughts will follow you all the way.

XXXI

I sense my limbs, for they are like branches in the air; the earth is as much my body as my bones.

XXXII

I will never stop dreaming of a better world; this is the direction of all thinking.

XXXIII

Humanity will never understand the visible universe, light, until it understands the invisible universe, consciousness.

XXXIV

Dreaming of sweetness, I awake to find myself eating bitter.

XXXV

Where is this unseen fountain which wells forth the spark of appearances?

XXXVI

Unseen, beneath the decadence of our great empire springs little flowers.

XXXVII

Mind centers motion.

XXXVIII

Although your face wanders in my heart, it is unknown to me; no wonder I cannot find you.

XXXIX

My body is space, my body is electric; in it I am free.

XL

The best I can do is to imitate greatness; through imitation I approach mirroring; in mirroring, I approach knowing.

XLI

Through inquiry I approach the ragged edge of my own barren structure and cannot find a way in, nor can I find a way out.

XLII

Youth is compression, old age—radiation. Life is contraction, death—expansion. The two, in their unfolding, constitute each moment of experience.

XLIII

The continuity of the mind is outside itself; so am I in your presence.

XLIV

The universe is the dynamic emission of the static union of sex paired opposites; in myself I am three.

XLV

All numbers, all diversity, all multiplicity, when taken together, constitute one; one alone constitutes zero by lack of comparison.

XLVI

Polarity is the chemistry of two; two, as inseparability, equals one; together two and one are three, and all three equals nine, multiplied in this three dimensional universe.

XLVII

In all humans, and in all beings, I see the divine dreaming, and I cherish that, for I, too, dream.

XLVIII

All fantasy is rooted in inadequacy; visualization is the perfection of these dull roots.

XLIX

All knowing is magnetic.

L

Creation is generosity; what is given must be balanced by equal regiving—all action stems from rest and seeks control through a return to balance.

LI

Every particle is centered in the whole limitless universe through the still light of presence; from each center extends the cycle of wave expressions of still light thinking.

LII

What I am you also are.

LIII

Divinity is one in cause and all in effect.

LIV

All that we know and cherish emerged from space; humanity itself is still in the making.

LV

There is nothing that the senses feel that the mind does not know simultaneously.

LVI

The universe is founded upon love; as such, neither human nor nation can survive fear.

LVII

The rhythms of nature are the ordained orbits of humanity; we can neither transcend them nor violate them.

LVIII

Wherever there is motion that motion is centered in stillness, which is its cause.

LIX

You cannot eat your own dying body.

LX

The Clear Light is invisible because it is always still; it becomes visible, through motion, as the five lights; it is felt as the rainbow body.

LXI

All matter desires to explode outwardly.

LXII

Humanity is still in the barbarian age of taking; our greatest lesson is to learn to give.

LXIII

With the quality of beginning, that which cannot be named creates God, the heavens, and the earth.

LXIV

Our concepts keep pace with our growth.

LXV

Polarity and sex are one—sex is the search for balance; this is universal.

LXVI

Union could not be possible without division; in this sense, the blessed experience of not-two contains the experience of two dividing and reuniting; this coming together is life; it is the spark of compassion.

LXVII

Bodies emerge from the womb to return to the source of all bodies.

LXVIII

Death is not negative life.

LXIX

All energy is tonal; all matter is frequency—the universe is sound emanating from still silence.

LXX

Senses can only reflect, they cannot know; the mind, being a sense door, also cannot know—only consciousness can do this.

LXXI

Our cultures belief in death has no validity, whatsoever, in nature.

LXXII

Humanity will not build an enduring civilization until it understands God; the history of popular religion is the history of misunderstanding God; we will not understand God until we understand light.

LXXIII

To know emptiness is to know how identity is retained, even when all things disappear, even when nothing arises.

LXXIV

The invisible can be known and comprehended in the same way that gravity can be known but never seen.

LXXV

Our cultures attempt to survive, to be happy, and to endure through violating the law of balance, the law of love; this cannot be done.

LXXVI

The reflections in any mirror are the reverse of their cause.

LXXVII

There is only a single experience which can be called unconditioned; we call this love—love alone is devoid of all purpose.

LXXVIII

Law is the symbol of truth; laws point beyond themselves to that which cannot be spoken—law belongs to delusion, truth to God.

LXXIX

Things are not held together from the inside, they are compressed together, like ice, from the outside through cold; all matter radiates the heat of sexual union that seeks emission.

LXXX

Creation is one thing—the division of equilibrium into equal sex pairs.

LXXXI

No two things can unite if they are pursuing opposite directions; union shows that division exerts in the same direction.

LXXXII

In reality, there is neither positive nor negative; one might as well say that there are two kinds of water, the kind that rises and the kind that falls.

LXXXIII

All bodies are electrical disturbances in a vacuum.

LXXXIV

Seven billion people can see the same event from seven billion different pin-points in space on this planet.

LXXXV

The universe cannot die; creation never began and will never end.

LXXXVI

It takes no effort to die; only life requires effort.

LXXXVII

In my body, I feel the great pulsing movement of the universe; I see the rain, and I weep.

LXXXVIII

All fire is flame; all flame is heat, all heat is radiation—
radiation is the principal of death; knowing this, I am free
of death fear, for the warmth of the heart is freedom; it is
the heat released from the bondage of compression.

LXXXIX

There comes a day when we begin to hear the Inner Voice.

XC

The answers I seek are dependent upon the length of time
it will take to know them.

XCI

The universe is desire; desire is our greatest power; the
tree growing around the shade, seeking the sun—there is
desire in this.

XCII

You create your own universe; each human being is a local
event universe.

XCIII

Motion simulates reality—this is the meaning of
appearance and emptiness.

XICV

The universe is the dramatization of love, expressed
through action and reaction, which are equal.

XCV

The path should be measured by freedom and love alone; against this standard, we know ourselves in our humility or lack thereof.

XCVI

All motion must have a fulcrum which does not move— when humanity understands this, we will transcend violence, hatred, and ill-will in that day.

XCVII

The universe is in perfect balance, a balance which cannot be disturbed by even one electron, for nothing can be outside it; knowing this my heart overflows.

XCVIII

Intuition tells me that there is no end to what I do not know; the same intuition tells me that all is knowable.

XCIX

Selflessness is the only freedom, emptiness the foundation of sanity.

C

Enlightenment is the manifestation of the presence of an absence.

CI

Seek values that lie within their source rather than seeking them in their shadows.

The Ritual of Fire and Light

Here, the chest heaves,
And the ragged land comes upon us,
As sky and cloud, under the Midnight Sun,
Open to blood and rage,
To the torrential anger
          Of our separation

          Into darkness,
Surrounded, from the inside out,
By the scream of ancient thoughts,
Echoing in the chamber
          Of great silence
          And immense stillness

How do we come to this rage?

Through endless jungles,
Anxious of time, here,
This journey is made alone,
And together, simultaneously

Here, in our shared experience,
We gather alone, around the ritual fire,
We gather alone, in the high desert night,
          And journey inward
Through self and other,
          To the source
Of our terrifying aggression

Those who make it here
Are intimate with aggression,
   With desire—
We must know this fire,
For it gave birth to us,
It forged the crucible
   Of suffering itself

Only those truly weary
   Come to this fire,
To this place at the center of things,
To this point of light

Only those who have learned it all
   And lived it thoroughly
Who have had it all collapse, only
To discover that the highest wisdom,
Is that they know nothing

Only those who have lived
Through endless cycles
   Of passion and aggression
Who are determined enough to emerge
From the jungle and open their eyes
To the confusion and thirst
That burns in the heart

Only those who understand
This precious human birth
   Come here

For few are capable
Of making the inner journey home

All come here in time,
But to be undone is the greatest
      Of human journeys,
And it is only through the fullness
      Of our humanity
That we can unwind this eternal knot
At the base of the soul
And open our awareness
To the primordial fire,
Which burns but gives no pain

From the depths of our shadow
We emerge to integrate
The full expression of our dual arising,
For the embodiment of our humanity
Is the fullness of divinity

And around the fire,
In the ritual of light,
In the stillness and silence
      Of complete surrender
We gather together to chant
And to rectify this manifestation,
This frozen energy, the imprisonment
      Of light in aggregate form

      Here, around this fire,
Which is everywhere, and every when,

In solitude, and in the mess of culture,
>We touch our source,
>The point of existence,
>And freedom is felt
>>It is lived

The Call

Like a candle wall
Against red flame
I become thin,
And through me,
The light begins to shine

Tired of computers,
Tired of consumption
The madness of this
Culture unchecked
Wears on and out, and the
Distraction, too,
>Burns up

>Stretched thin,
I am joyous
And yet sick to death
Of this contraction,
Of this resistance to Life
And as the heat
Of this inner fire grows,
The sound of Loving Awareness

Calls from the blue deep
And resounds, infinite and clear,
Wearing thin—this pain

Before, I could not hear you
Nor of what you ask of me
But now, you are clear
It is clear—that courage is
The only response to life

The courage to release,
To let go of what is beyond
Controlling, and to follow
The flow, back to the center
Of this sunlit sky, where
You sound and echo, like laughter,
The call of human freedom
To become full of Life
To speak, to act, to shine
And boom forth your fullness
From the empty depths
Of a being far beyond me
Like an ancient drum,
In the open air

I smell the fragrance
Of ceremony, and
I hear the call of silver bells
And I am blessed,
For the purpose of my life
Is finally clear—may I radiate

Compassion—may my personality
Display wide open and free
Like clear light through a
Clear crystal gem
May my life be a loving
Display of Essence so that
I may develop complete acceptance
    And openness
    To all situations,
    To all emotions,
    And to all beings

Part III
As I Am

2011-2012

"...I AM THE fool of this story, and no rebel shall hurl me from my throne..."

—G.K. Chesterton

As I Am

What is history?
Other than story
What lies between light and dark?
An endless array
A vast shifting emptiness
From the spoke
Of one wheel

This is me
As I am

In the oncoming storm
The cloud, the rocky skyline
Above the mountain fades back

And standing in the shadow
Of a thousand questions
Is me again
With nothing at all to say

The questions never leave me
But each is my own
Telling me in my own words

Simply,
Not to
Want

So much

Another and Another and Another

Another and another and another

If I am the one who stands
In this waking dream
The man who walks
The same narrow steps
Again, and again
Only to find himself the same
Only to face the closing door
Of every man's desire
Devotion—what is given so freely by one
And denied just the same to another
Stripped from the bare and aching hands
Of one who may not be worthy
In the eyes of what forever lies
In some unknown realm
The seed crushed and scattered
To the ends of a promised day
Always before the light
Has even a chance
To warm its virgin skin

If I am this man
Then what if I may ask
Is the question
I cannot seem to answer

Who is this man I cannot be?
A man who fills the void
Of another's wants

The riddle so many find with joy, so easy
Tomorrow and tomorrow and tomorrow
And another and another and another
Again, and onward into the will
Into the dimming light of that tomorrow
Clung and held against the heart
So tight and cherished by so many

The companion of the unknown day
The vision of perfection
So clear and sweet
To the mind not yet crippled
By a truth too heavy to look in the eyes
Yet bearing down on shoulders
Already steady beneath their only earth

I know, I have so many
Images of myself
And of others
Please...I know
I know I have so much
That I have built inside

So much that the truth
Is afraid to let itself be shown
This I know, we carry so much with us
Through each day
Without the lightness
Without a song
To bridge the sorrow

And yet, I know that in each fertile center
There sleeps a seed
That carries with it
Tomorrow and tomorrow and tomorrow
Each one a different face
A different story strung along
In endless lines

Who is this man you want me to be?

He is not the perfect picture
Who fits into frames
He is not what cannot be
He is what he is
And can be nothing else
For he is just like every man
Who has seen behind the façade
Every one of us that has drawn aside the veil
And trembled at our own uncertain face
And stood strong in the light of the mind
And screamed into the distant black, draped in fear
Screamed—I will not become lost in it all
Lost to some concept

I am not afraid
And I will not accept
That I am not enough
Today, I heard and faced
The worst of myself in situations
Almost frequent enough to be called laws
In a jungle, looming alien
Above and winding in from all sides

I faced concepts that told me
In no uncertain terms
There will always be
Another and another and another
To tell you that you are not enough
But know that in every fertile center
There sleeps a seed
And even from something so small
Can grow something mighty

The Places We Are

If only, I could understand
The place I am now
There are so many of us
Lost in the places we are

Each step sinks
Into the ground below
Climbing a ladder to nowhere

There will always be
A world beyond
Something to be
Someone to become
A hidden treasure
On the other bank of the river

But perhaps, we are not
As complicated as we think
Maybe, it is all a weaving of smoke
And none of this is at all serious

When those rare times come
And the pressure of life subsides
When for once my eyes
Open to the strangeness
To the wonder, I blink
And sigh, and laugh a little, and wish
For the simple sake of sanity—

If only we could understand
The places we are now

The Space Between

Last night, I dreamt that I had died
    For a while

    The end came

And in that brief moment
The space between
    A breath
The life left in me became vast
Without shape or size or time
One by one, the impressions
Of a life running parallel
With all lives
Reflected in the light of a distant mind
Enveloped as a drop in the eternal ocean

And the me that I knew
The center from which all my life swung
Faded into the back
And all I held so dear
All I took for granted
Became small and bled through into
The divine current running
Beneath and behind all things

Darkness set in—then light
And then, it all became clear
And empty and free

And then, I knew what it was like to exist
Without a center, as the real me
The clear light, the void, the ocean
The radiant source that cannot die
Because it was never born

But all that is words
And what I am
      Is not

And in this place
In that brief moment
What felt like a thousand lifetimes
Became nothing more
Than the space between a breath
And I was pulled back to life
Pulled back into my dream

Last night, I dreamt that I had died

      For a while

And in the end
None of it at all mattered
None of my story
Nothing of my sadness
Not an ounce of my beliefs

And now in this waking life
I walk in those spaces
Between all the small things
And I do not worry about death
For as someone much smarter than me once said
Whoever does not know how to die
And come back to life
Is but a sorry traveler
On this dark earth

Amores (I)

For all that I have never had
I sing to you in silent fear
That all this beauty and passion in me
Will wither and go unused

With the best of my heart and mind
For all I could ever dream of
      Please, I ask of you—
Just give me one full moment of life expressed

To breathe with you as one
And bury my head within
For all I do not have and everything you are

      This light in me shines
And I stand tall with open arms and eyes
Ready to receive this greatness within you

In a Divided Sea

      It appears
I keep building for us a house
In some future that lies only inside my head
Silent, in between every thought, you weave
In and out, and walk softly towards me
With the grace of what could never happen
For in the realm of what does happen
Exists no such room for you and me, or so it seems

We were forced apart before we even met
By the cruel and narrow
Grip of thought
And I doubt you even know this
For your eyes do not speak ill
But only of distance
And the unwilling smile
That decided not to let me in, to push me away
For the sake of another, the sake of circumstance
Will always intrude and keep from me
The love that I desire

It will never cease to amaze me
How fast hope can turn to pain
How fast a smile and open arms
Can become a wall between two
With so much room to grow and expand
Into the warmth of relationship

With so much hurt
I fear that I will always remain
A man in a divided sea
Divided against the growth, the potential
Flowing forth from me in passing dreams
And shameful glances down

A gateway to what remains clothed in mystery
So simple, yet so hard for others to see
Why else could such a love remain chained?

Some days, I wish that we had never met

Then I would not have to walk in this world
With the knowledge that there is one like you
Out there beyond my reach
And I know, that this seems as if it could only come
From the lower realms
But remember what sleeps beneath every oak
All things must grow before they decay
And every shell must break for life to come forth

So, with this I know that I must leave it all behind
And face you with my head held high
But I cannot continue to wish and hope
And dream any longer
A man cannot live on a smile alone
The menu is not the meal
And a heart so strong cannot support itself forever

With all the heartache that could ever happen
For all that may never be
Know that even though I do not really know you
I love you, and perhaps
One day, we can build a house
Together in a mind and soul united
And walk together in grace
Within the realm of something real
Forged in the embrace of what I have longed for

True Home

A subtle smell
On the warm evening breeze
Opens the door to another world
   Within this one
And the veil draped across
The height of potential in every day
   Drifts in and out
And comes to me in silent drops

The warmth in me radiates through
From this stage to the next
With only a brief
Yet thunderous glimpse
Of the enormity
Abandoned to the hands
Of each of us in each moment
To see the lightness and frivolity

The responsibility to ourselves
To know that we are not the victims
   Of forces beyond
That we are not helpless puppets
At the mercy of fate and chance
That our voice echoes through the end

In tears, I see through my own games
And with a crash of thunder
I come together at the seams
And all my tragic life is lost

With the laughter to the swelling tide
Found at once in my true home

Images of Me

    Sometimes,
When the weight is bearing down
When the life I build
Becomes too much to understand
When so many of my creations
Take on a will and twirl
       And race
       Within the mind
       All at once
       From all directions

Without reason, without form, without meaning

    Sometimes
In one swift moment
These eyes are taken back
And all the ends of this
Created life
Become clear and sharp, opening before me
Like a chill ocean wind

    Sometimes,
      In this clarity
Something strange and new begins to form
      An image

Of myself, as I actually am
Always wanting
Always asleep through each step
Across a constructed and careful world
Laid before me by my own hands
    Tired hands
Already old, before their time
Yet never as old as all the ones
That lay my foundations

    Sometimes,
I can see another image
Reflected against itself
Off and going into the eternal distance
Each one a different face
Of the same man
A dream intertwined
With the ruin of what I cannot remove
From this world we all share

    Sometimes
This man can soar and reach the heights
Of what could only be a dream
And sometimes he is close
And may even begin to walk in your world
The closer he gets to this world
The more of a ghost I become
The I constructed by all the weight
Of all the past, of all the time
    Of all the future

I cannot release, cannot let go
Even from these tired hands

      Sometimes
When the mind becomes a maze
I cannot sift through
When all that I create whirls around me
Like an ocean wind
I remember, and for a moment
I stand outside
And look in at what is
And always will be an image

Round and Round

And so, it goes, round and round
Of all the seeds of pain
The world gives me
None can compare
To the weight I place
On my own shoulders

Running and running
The same day appears
Or so it seems to lazy eyes
And the mind that has grown
Too tired to remain in a clench upon itself
As if thinking made me exist

And so, it goes, round and round

Down cavernous depths
Of leftover dreams and half thunk thoughts
Spilling from the other world into this one
Fooling me to think that one day
All of this will make
Some kind of sense

But it will not, and I am nothing but tired
      Tired of waiting
      Tired of pretending
And so now, the strings will dance for no one
A no one who must move on to the next game
      And so, it goes
And like the clock it only goes 'round
      Until it turns no more

You

      Rolling eyes
      Sliding hands
      Across the hips
Twinkling in the mind's eye
So many pictures of you
Drawing me close

In so little that we have
I must bring myself to laugh
For although the future weighs heavy

Upon us, and all I have of you
Is in dreams and hope, still

The soft touch of those lips
And those bright blue eyes
The feel of you so close
And still so far from me
Like the striking distance between
That I do not understand

I have never met a one like you

The warmth you radiate
The way you reflect in all those around you
The best of ourselves
Just wanting and wishing that perhaps
In some fleeting day
You could see yourself in me
And draw me close and breathe together
Collapsing in the warmth of our acceptance
As two sides of one love

Retail Clerk

For all the years spent
In cold dark places, dirty
Rotten, with hands in-between
Metal and wire, cramped
In coffins stuffed with boxes
From corporations with eyes closed to reality

Built on the backs
Of some of the smartest people I have ever met
And some of the dumbest, but
People nonetheless

After all the years
All the tired faces
All the stories of hands and the deep night
For all the humanity I have seen
And all the injustice
I sing a song for all in you that has been silenced
And all that is born

For all the years spent
Breathing the damp air
Of coolers and metal tombs, cavernous
A dungeon too familiar to be called harsh
Flickering lights and that odd faint smell of milk
Battered knees and wrists
Twisted skin and weathered hands
Minds clenched in repose to some madness
Far beyond common sense

In my memory, I am filled
With corridors and isles
Monstrous machines
Bright hospital lights and endless cardboard
Glass and plastic enough to choke
The god itself

In the beginning, you spoke with the voice
Of America in the days before
The industrial complex
The bright smiling face of the neighborhood
And the dream of prosperity rolling in
Shiny with new labels and that slick factory sheen
But then came the shift
And what was contained became unwieldy
Unbridled and fierce
The wave too big for itself spilled over
With money and the consuming vacuum of human greed
And the lives of all those invested
Went down in spirit

I came in with so many of those lives
Riding the end of that wave
And was lucky enough to make it just before
You truly died to those just trying to make it now

For years, I climbed a ladder that led nowhere
Except headless, through a sea of dust and rusted metal
And I would tell myself
That I was torn from sleep
If I could kid myself that I ever slept
Birthed in shadows into all hours of the night
Riding through ghost towns
So early it was the day before
Ready to bury my hands into cold
And squeeze myself thin
Between doors, walls, and boxes
Thanking god I am not claustrophobic

Ready to stand on knees
And stay there
And run from here to there
Twisting and turning to be in
Three places at once
Remembering that in all the
Effort, in all the uncommon nonsense
Is nothing but food and simple human
Necessity crammed inwards
Behind plastic and foil skin
The honesty of the human condition
Exploited, wealth confused with money
And driven downwards into the spirit
Of those behind impersonal speakers
Those behind the paychecks
Pushing from all angles to force
A robotic image of a human being
Uniformed, scripted, and blind

And we became that
In the third of our day—
One to sleep, one to work, one for what we will
We gave in with all the might
Of those starving and ready to be happy
Ready to be given our slice of humanity
In scales of a thousand hours

Punching keys, filling lives with useless products
Of a useless age
Each day like the last
Noise and movement from all around

Busy, busy, busy, beep, beep, beep
Funny how each day felt the same
With so much change all around
Ink and paper, transactional greet
On you go, next and next and next
Bagging your life into paper or plastic
Faces and name tags come and go
Summer job, youth and grownup adolescents
Trying to find something
To keep themselves afloat
Some stick with it and chain themselves to the scale
To the promise of a wage almost good enough
To be second class

Once there was a time when we where
In league with the rest of them
The dying breed, the old school
Mentors and old timers, lifers
The face of a dead profession
Killed off by Wal-Mart and the new contract
Never enough to pass a union vote

Tired, again and again
The same story played itself out
Jaw clenched, I buried myself under
The unfinished, the almost enough
And took on so much, too much—
Become the workhorse
In league with only a few
That walked in the shadows
Of the night, working while all others slept

Responsible for what?
I still don't know
To keep the game going
To supply the public staples
And smile in the face of disaster

For years, between working for dreams
Trying to fit myself into my own boxes
Labels defining who or what?
Some prize down the road
Shining on a pedestal
Ready to be placed further down the line
Along with all the other dreams
Of a day without the pressure
Of trying to fight the change
Building castles in the sand
Before the tide, knowing everyday—
The tide is coming

For years, I pushed on into the change
Hoping that maybe one day it would be different
That one day we would give up the stupidity
The impossible fight against the change

Environment changes, people change
Even work changes a little
But on and on it goes
The same dance upon a worn-out stage

For all the years spent
On my knees and staying there

For all the faces, all the stories
All the humanity
For all the hands cramped between
Shit and wire
In spaces too small for human hands
But just right for packaged food
I stand and sing a song for all in you that has died
And all that is born

For although you weighed heavy upon me
And all the countless others
It is in you that I was forged
Like iron, birthed in pressure
To go singing through the world

Clumsy

The early light of the afternoon sun
Glitters and dances across the open page
            Of my life
And deep within, an exquisite
Moment of clarity is willing itself into being
Trying to show me, trying to guide me
To that place beyond the borders of myself
Where the simple fact can blossom
In that early expanding light
From the sun of another life

The fact that I, if I may dare admit
Take myself too seriously

And all this visceral combative force of emotion
Is nothing but my own misguided thought
Daring the disgusting notion
Of wanting the one above the many

Pulled along, carried away down avenues
Through so many open doors
I fall over my own feet
Like a clumsy ball of silly feelings
Gathering trash along the way
With ears open to a busy world
The voice of story reveals to me
The truth of all stories—
That each one must have an author
So, if in fact I am the author of my own woes
Then I am the fool of this story
And no one, no rebel
Shall hurl me from my throne

A Well Inexhaustible

Like all people
I have no past
And no future
No, what I have is only now
And together, we may draw upon
A past that is shared
The world has past
And the world is people
And our story is told

By all those who see
That in the people
Through them, through us
It is more than life itself
It is one life, one story, one hero
With a thousand faces
And through that story
      I become a well
      Inexhaustible
With tears that filled the oceans
And parted the sky and earth
And loved with so many
Each set of hands, every bleeding vein
That carries the past along
Both sides of the human being
United in forgiveness
I turn to face the unknown
Armed with a story untold
Being written in each step
With faith in the missing half of myself
Without fear for the story
That has not yet been written

Diamond Mind

The only thing I want
Is human freedom
Not a freedom defined
And conditional
Boxed in ideas

About ideals, within
Concepts and forgotten dreams
Wishes and hopes
But a freedom inside
The freedom to be still
And let all that arises
Truly pass away, untouched

I want the freedom
To be quiet
And stride through life
      Let go
Adrift in a sea of change
With nothing
But clear eyes
And a radiant diamond mind

Free from every passing whim
Free from every attempt
At becoming better
And above all, free from my self

What is freedom?
But letting go
Of what should be
And opening eyes to what is

Alone

Alone,

The rain beats on sunken rooftops
And the faint sound of cars
Passing into the distance
Persists into the early spring evening
And somewhere behind
The clouds the moon shines

Alone,

In some quiet humming room, dim
Above empty shops and abandoned streets
Someone sits for a thousand springs
And between shadow and light
The momentum, like a train
Out of the past, unwinds

Alone,

He lets all the heavy years
Trailing behind him
Like the wake of a ship
Break apart and dissolve
For in this moment, he sees
Himself for perhaps the first time

Alone,

As he has always been
Nothing out of the past
Has made him, no names
No history or pain
No books or words or culture
And above all—no god

Alone,

He feels lost; he runs in the dark
Back and forth in empty buildings
And he never finds the right door, but tonight
The light behind the sky, even in the long night
Gives him peace and the sense
That one day he will not be

Alone,

And that all will come together
Like beads on one string
Uniting him with a lonely other
Descending the crest of a living wave
Accepting all that shapes the days
Like a train out of the past

Alone

Explaining a Few Things

Excuse me,
To spit on the feet
Of high minded romantic
Notions, floating in and out
Of the ridiculous, circumstances
Beyond the ordinary
And too far beyond
Any sense I can make

Let me unwind all
The unkind words about my
Character and
Explain a few things

Why do we feel ourselves to be
        So complicated?
Why weave ourselves, our lives
Our opinions about love
        And loss
Into so many useless dimensions?

Why carry so many burdens
So much baggage
Around with us? so much past
And wear our masks
When meeting each day
The face of another's sorrow
My own face
Confronting yours

Love, in my eyes
Is a simple thing
And for years, I have watched
The dancing masks, actors
Fools and maybe even a few
Honest souls
Pervert something simple
With stuttering nonsense
Trailing behind like ribbons in the wind

Perhaps, I ask too much of others
To meet each moment new
Without our delusions
To know the real me, the real us
Is not something deep and far away
Not something bitter and or hidden
Between the lines
Of some story you tell
But here, in the way we are

Where do we get this notion
That we are the story
Trailing behind us?

For when I take the time to look
With the right set of eyes—
Open, all I see is what is before me

And each word is the first
The first step is the last

Each breath is the only
And all I am is the happening

So then, from where does all the mystery come?
Why does the sting of unanswered questions
Linger and swell the heart beyond bursting?
It is only in the story, trailing behind us

Silly Questions

Can this moment be clean and free
Of residue from the past?
Words, echoing in the head as mere noise
      Stop, look, listen
Moments of arising, grasped in the palm of the mind
Between the All and Emptiness
Only a difference of name, and how
To look at myself as if I were someone else?
And so, to look at others as being myself
      Seeing the end of time
The journey inward to the eternal home
Within and throughout the silent black

The past is only a memory
The future—anticipation
Ideas, concepts, fractured and split
Between a thousand dusty mirrors
Ghosts of language and grammar
An endless play of patterning
Projected through the human game

Wild before the feelings of a self
Misplaced and distant from the senses

The bell rings clear and loud
The sound echoes and fades back
Into all sound, the one energy behind the many
The pebble falls into rough waters
Smoothed with a flatiron
Sending rings out in unison through the shaken mind
　　　Left alone, the water stills
And the rings leave no residue on the water's surface

Altars of Pride

Memory upon memory
Scarred upon the skin, the
Altar of pride, stained by
Everything which comes raining
Out of forgotten mouths
Blending together
Like foam on broken waves
Fantasy becomes too real to handle
And out of the present act
I come running in tears
With all the rest
Towards a familiar hoax
Buried in the outstretched distance
Lost in the pride

Naming, labeling, defining
The boarders between us
I stand in the presence
Of so many walking bags of memories
Molding myself out of so much
Forgotten talk, always listening
To the subtle beliefs
The assured walk of all those people
Who manage to fool themselves
Into believing truly
In whom they are
Building bridges in innocence
With all the memories upon
   Memory
Burned into skin like altars
Etched in hollow lakes of pride

Responsibility

Here we stand together, regardless
With eyes open, or not
To the same cries
Echoing from a center of weakness
Shrinking back into painful corners
Afraid to stand tall against the oncoming light
   And say with certainty—

   "I did it! I am responsible!"

Shoulders throughout the world
Join in supporting this burden
The weight of all the mistakes, of years
Upon years of narrow forward thinking
Action without awareness
The paradox of responsibility
Moving in equal sway throughout
All the ten directions
Heading swift and strong into the space
In front and behind us, eyes that can only
Look in one direction
Like eyes in the mirror that
Never seem to move

We stand at the center, together
Life flowing into us from every angle
And gushing out in more ways than we can see
Affecting so much, from the atom to the face
Passing us in the street with an averted gaze
   Walking through tunnels
In private spheres, cut off, alien, alone
Strangers in this world
   And to ourselves
Wayward spirits in bags of skin
Ghosts in the machine

The warming world around us
Changing fast, despite our disconnection
Never stopping to consider our delusions
Barreling forward in equal reaction
   Without being shoved

Force without a forcer
Doing without a doer
Karma without blame
A world without a plan for the better

Here at the center of a screaming earth
Naked and vulnerable
Is me—I alone did it
I am everyone who looks away
I am the weakness inside
Burning deep behind the eyes
Forcing us to turn away our hearts and minds
From all that we commit in weakness
And I am you
Eyes fixed in the mirror
Unable to look away

This is me, this is us
Taking the first and last step
To look and only look
And so see ourselves
Remaining still and quiet
In the howling wind of change
And perhaps not trying to fix it
Making things worse, knowing
That the quiet is all we need

A World Without

I tried to start a revolution once
      It failed

Picture a world with an orange sky
Picture a world without oceans
A world without trees

Picture our world without cities and cars
Without computers and money
Picture our world without presidents
Congress, ambassadors, or police

Let me tell you about the world I see

You're standing in an office building
The floor is covered in moss and leaves
And the sun shines through the clouds
Revealing a maze of decimated buildings
Torn open and completely overtaken
      By vines and life
Pools of water collect in abandoned stores
And the ruins of a shopping center are now home to a
Family of dark skinned people
With braided hair and leather clothes

Ninety percent of the world's plant life
Has gone extinct in the past two thousand years
      Imagine it coming back

Picture a world without rules
A world without leaders

Because there are not enough people left to care

You're standing in an abandoned highway
And you walk past rusted cars
With flat tires and broken windows
You look over the railway
The ocean stretches out for miles
And the air is clean and free of smog and exhaust

Picture a world without religion

Without messiahs
Or holy books written by people who died
Two hundred generations before you were born
You do not have a job or a title
You are not obligated to do anything but survive
You do not know what America was
Nor do you care

You have never heard of Jesus Christ

At night, you can see more stars
Than on the clearest night in 2004
You hear stories of the ancient world
But it is shrouded in mystery
And nothing makes any sense

You're standing under a tree
That has grown out of the cement
Of an abandoned parking lot
Grass and moss have burst
     From the ground
And you fall asleep under this benign growth

You wake up and its 2005
And you're working sixty hours a week
     To survive

Distraction

Always lurking, tying the veil
The greatest of our miseries
And yet our only consolation
For all the desire
Turning to shadow in our hands
Forced into movement
For it is unbearable for us
     To sit still

The highest form of activity is rest

With eyes closed, I can see
Perfection just beyond the moving forms
Blurred into a thousand shapes and thoughts
Moving from one fractured word to the next
Like a monkey in a cage

Funneled out of memory
Into the river of anticipation

Fire under the legs, demanding me to stand
What brings me into this room?
Only to lead me astray

It will always be you
Itching at the center of bones
From one flashing noise to the next
Filling me with partial thoughts
Shifting beneath the veil, drawing it closed
Shrinking the aperture
Through which the universe looks at itself
Waiting, always waiting, for the perfection in rest

Cruel Joke

Two

      Beautiful

             Women

         Once said

To me

        "...Any girl would be lucky

To have you..."

And if that

Is true

It is a

Cruel joke

Impermanence

The trust of hands in faith
To all that expands and contracts
With the wind of awareness
Examining the truth of all life
Like a microscope into the living body
Collapsing into the unknown

The end of busyness
Converging in tension
The mind adrift in a sea of its own creation
      This too must pass
And dissolve with each stone
We lay together upon the foundation
Of human ignorance
Turning our backs, again and again
To the glaring truth
Revealed in the plain and simple fact
      Of all experience

That even matter is relevant
And what is solid
Is in fact spacious, containing multitudes
Of distance and relation
Standing with one another
As planets to stars
And atoms to quarks
Life as it seems being nothing
But one radiant source
Pulsing within and out
Arising and passing away

Streaming across the spectrum
And falling in rhythm
To the empty floor
With neither shape nor size
Weight nor age to gage itself against
The heights of human thought
Prepared in all circumstance
To rally as one against the notion
That every idea we gather as one mind
Is false and impartial
Incomplete if it remains
A belief, a ground on which to battle
        Against death
And so rage against birth
And all the brilliance of life that lay between

Where there is expression
Of the great source, there can be no up
        Without down

And no clinging to what will fade
  And wither
Where there is understanding
There is not pain but only an experience
That moves and changes
And arises only to pass away
   In an endless dance

If I am alive I am also dead
  And if I am both
  I am neither
  If I am neither
  I am nothing
  And if I am nothing
I am all that sees us together
In trust, riding upon the hands of faith
To all that expands and contracts
With the choiceless wind of awareness

In the Slime

No time but the present
Yet never the right time
For me, for us
For any of the ones
I find within this pale ugliness
Of my own experience

Dirty streets, long worn out by useless ideals
And useless people with no ambition

The long night passes cold and unnoticed
     And here I sit, alone
     At the same old table
Across from an empty chair
With an empty longing for an unknown what?

Out of the echo of so many deceitful faces
Comes yours, with a soft and gentle voice
Quiet and hidden, beneath a noisy inner room
Fading in and out of the shimmering vision
Of myself lost in the wake
Of the same old feelings
And the same old questions

This biting empty hole of my life
     A familiar failure
The unsuccessful courtship
Never able to assure myself, like all the others
Into believing that my mistress isn't there
Yet seeing you reflected in the slime

Shame covering my smile
If only I could ask for you
To take this longing from me
And bury it deep within your own past
And so, see yourself through my eyes and
See me shining in a new and different light

Maybe then might you take me in your hands
And show me that if only once
My heart did not lead me into the den of pain

Frustration and heartache, headlong into
An image, sitting in an empty chair
A thought in place of a feeling
Then maybe, I could forget
That it isn't really you that I long for
If only once my love did not stand alone
I could leave it all behind
And seek truly the light in the darkness
Of the poet's dream

So once again, sitting here in the long night
Across from endless empty chairs
Is me saying that I need a break
From being brushed aside
And ignored like I don't feel
With the might of a thousand suns

Perhaps one day there will be time
For me, for us
And maybe one day, we will remember
That there is no time but the present
And that this, this is the right time
For no longer can I remain lost

Searching in the slime
For something real

Amores (II)

Deep inside, I know I am at fault
For wanting all my dreams to converge
In some world other than the full
And open wish I keep inside

For wanting you to be real
And walk in the same pathless land
With origins of a different heart
Without this pain of knowing

That every one of you will leave
That all the beauty, longing, and grace
Will pass me by without a glance

I know, deep within—I am at fault
For wanting you, above all else
My living dream, my dying muse

Romance

    At the end of life
How curious, we all look back
To dream of all we should have done
And all we wished we'd been

The path is stark and wide
Yet all the days of light and cloud
Vine and earth, heavens and rock

The mountain beyond the crag
Lay distant, gone from the weary
          Searching for a gate
Extinguished from the entrance
To the mouth of an unknown God

The titans lay waste the earth
For all those who wish only
To scale the heavens
And ascend in truth
To the Isis behind the veil

At last the afternoon star
Shines bright in the summer sky
And if only I could bring myself
To place one heavy foot
Upon the winding path
And release the burdens of this long
And fearful life

          To climb inward
And wish with so many for the strange
And awful lie of perfection

          Truth
Has not been found untrue
Truth has been found too difficult
And it has been left untried
Lost to the busy world of wind
In the towering empty city
Of human ease and thought

At the end of life
How many of us do not regret?
How many can pass the night
In rest without the passion
Of so many faded dreams?
So much left undone
And even more so
Left untried

The tale of all we should have been
The blood in each well
Has filled to the brim and spilled
Out upon the desert land
Of the lonely ones

And now, before the island sinks
Into the shifting sand
Laying deep into the bed of stone
      And fire
The path is split wide
If only the brush and vine
Would burn and turn to ash

For all those who wish only
To scale the heavens and ride
With angels to the gates of another earth
I ask with heavy feet to leave nothing here
      Undone

Introvert

How can I begin to explain
         The mystic art
By which the quiet soul
Is intricately bound?
And how each pilgrim before me
Can by knowledge of the infinite
Face the low and misguided vision
Of ourselves in the ears
Of all the loudness?

By the education we choose
To undertake to stabilize the vision
The screaming inner voice
And enter communion
         With the real

How by the strength of all I cannot say
Am I to stand amongst the crowds of chatter?
And ride the wave of the eager
Into the rigid center of all you deem important
         In this human life?

The exquisite pain by which we live
In each moment unable to bridge the gap
Between our inmost selves
Across the striking distance between
Even the most ordinary of things
And the overwhelming depth
Of so much disregarded feeling

For so long, we remain alone inside
Wanting nothing more than to echo
Across the chasm that surrounds us
And show the world the wealth
Uncovered in the stillness
Within each of us
Masked by a constant stream
Of inner noise

Sometimes, we scream
So loud that no one hears
And sometimes, we are quiet
Through and through
To the clear and vibrant core
From where all thought springs
Like water from an empty pitcher

For in that deep and welcome silence
We come face to face
With ourselves, and all the painted words
Drip from the surface
Of a dust free canvas
A mirror that receives
But does not keep

And we are not ashamed
Although the world may like us to be
The questions speak freely of it
They breathe unacceptance—
Why are you so quiet?

And to this I can only say—
I do not have an answer
That is not silence
All I have is the difference between
Thunder and lightning
And that is enough for now

A Song

When the day was new again
Down came the brittle walls of the stone sun
And the garden rushed to meet the open hand
    When the years lost
Collected in silent windows
They with all the rest were blind
And taken away into the steep night

    And we forgot
The story as we murmured
Amongst the dreaming
Playful glace, the eye
In all the death and woeful blue
With some who hear the ocean breathe
And go in lines with all the rest
What speech is said for all the lost
That gives us here an open meaning
To a nonsense playful pure

Devoid of structure in the sense
Of time to clear the eye of doubt

The mind beneath the weighted breast
An altar raised in steady glide

On the wayfarer walks, on sand
And stone and sun baked hands of clay
Frozen in an endless dancing
Play for all the working gods
Again, we find the answer clear
The storm cloud drains its hidden want

And we forgot the way we were

The Circle

Freeing the circle, bound
In solid sadness lines, around
The broken form, beyond the frame
Of someone searching still

A fullness inside, untouched
Yet believing always
In all the tears
Seeping in through lightness cracks
In the wilted sky

Perhaps, I am not alone
In my disinterest, my distance
Not wanting like so many
To flutter from one excitement
        To the next

To charge with all my might
To the shores of something shallow
Brief and fleeting

But to wait and do my best
To be still in my eyes
And ready for openness
      In my heart
And solidarity in the will
        Of another

After all the patterns of denial
I have only lost a little of my faith
Just enough to fracture
Me into a thousand men
Each with his own longing
Now splintered across
The empty spectrum of my life

A thousand sets of eyes peering
In at one lovely face
Unchanging for now
Yet bound to change

In time, each piece of the key
Will fit its rightful place
And send tremors along the fulcrum
Through the deep structure
Of my weird little universe
And like each time before

You will push me away slowly
    And for good

The circle grows and shrinks
Yet it never changes shape
And all this searching in me
Has brought me inexplicably to you

And so here I stand, ready, bound
With a fullness preserved
If not for a little faith left
To be restored

With hope tested against the grain
In the wake of bitter chance
And the power of secret will
That in love you could gather me
    One by one

And at last free me
From this endless circle

Chatterbox

The essential way flows everywhere
So how can it require practice?
The breeze dances with me open and light
To find myself again facing a wall—
    Navel gazing

The breath slows and becomes heavy
Sinking inwards dripping warm
At the back of the throat
And I too become like a ball of molten iron
And delve within for a taste of the unborn
Eyelids unsure, fixated bellow the belly center
      Open close in out

Who is it that hears? Attention!
      It is breathing me
      And off I go
Just as soon as I begin to settle
Out of the back of the mind
Like a wave, it comes

Memories etched into leaves fluttering about
Flapping like a banner in the wind
"It is only your mind that flaps"
And then I remember
I brought a support through this door
And silly me, I discarded it seven thoughts back

Off and back again—
That is the profession
Of the sitting chatterbox

Amores (III)

Around you, the heart beats wild in cage
And away runs the mind in want

For something so simple
As to hold you—skin to skin

    And feel the core of you
Forgetting, if only once, this lonely ache
In the deep and endless corridor
That runs in all hopeful directions within me

    To a center nowhere
And to a future never so wrong as this—
A man divided, hurt, and as always, far too eager

A bewildered stranger, even to myself
Forever holding on to what
If not the impossible dream of you

Nothing to Do

Despite all the chaos
I can never be blessed with enough
Nothing for me to do

This monument lies grand and towering
In the vast distance of barren land
Between the here and the there
A shining pedestal in the future eye

Complete action sets my feet in motions
Beyond the simple reason of today
For it seems this mountain has already been climbed

By countless a one before the day
I dared to dream of it myself
And all this savage drought
Through which I must pass
      Seems all but useless
To the jester with nothing to do
      And nowhere to go

With nothing new under an old and dying sun
And all I could ever dream of saying
Waiting for me in the mouths of others
What room is there for my lunatic ravings?
And foolish dreams of walking in league
With all but the greatest of my teachers?

And then if hits me—the obvious fact
That each generation is the first and only
And everything said can and must be said again
      Clear and simple
For all the deaf that wander through life asleep
And for all those who cannot be bothered to care
For anything not bound in the tender delusion
      Of that shining happiness
      Somewhere down the line

      Who among us is not guilty?

So, count me then among the sleepwalking mass
And sign my name across the stars
Etched forever in the crude and awkward maps
Lighting the furrowed way

Across those barren lands
      To the liars lair

To a place where I can remain
Absorbed in myself with eyes sharp
Focused in like a river
That flows in no direction
Consumed by the fantasy of becoming
Filling my empty sack of being
With the burden we call knowledge
The prison built high without doors
Yet full of open windows that leer
Upon an unmistakable reality

     So again, I ask
What use is the barren land?
Between the here and the there
What room is there for one who knows
That there is nowhere left to go
And nothing left to pursue?
That those who live one day fully
Can die content in the evening
And welcome the blessing
Of all this nothing to do

Words

Heavy clunky words
Brutal and rigid
Frozen in time

How to describe
With such clumsy
Nonsense the delicate
Subtle verse of the
Mind universal

The empty hand

The breeze over the water's edge
The bells in the unknown distance
An afternoon so light
I cannot help but float
Just above the ground

The secret of light
Refracted in the wave
The humming trees
Full of color and sound

How do we presume
To capture truth
In a box that will not change?

When words fail, there is only
The sound of the rain
And all that moves
In the summer's wind

Happiness

Happiness is like a great symphony

It is beautiful, full of energy and life

Yet, it has a beginning, a middle, and an end

Peace is like the great silence

It was there before the symphony started

Its presence brings out the beauty

Of the symphony as it is being played

And it persists long after the symphony is over...

As We Are

From beginning to beginning
Like an empty page, dreary and secret amongst
The ebbing sea of an endless mind
Unfolding slow and strange
Before story and earth began
Tears in the sky beat softly
On concrete slabs
Before the road of an untold life

Stilted in some drifting autumn wind
The painted hero approaches
Step by step, ascending the great ladder
With common feet and an uncommon sense
Long arms reaching out of the past
To a cold and bitter moon

Dredging along an unknown street
Before the throne of slain leaders
Hovering vast above the heads
Outreached, in weary cries
A voice strong and clear echoes
Throughout the people's song
And from the beginning
Shook with thunder to the deep places
    Of the universe

    And piece by piece
The notions of a united heart
Came together in a spirit unyielding
If only to say with a voice collected
From shards of wheat and stone
    That this is us—
    As we are

We are wiggly and diaphanous
Like the outline of the morning hill
A dance of nerves in the common brain
We do not fit into boxes and straight lines
And no amount of force will
    Make us good

And together, each one of us a hero
We walk through unknown streets
Sunken in invisible cities
A parade throughout time
Banners filled with blood and dirt
A canvas painted with all the truths
The dead need spoken now
      And without shame
For all is past and memory

      From end to end
Pages torn from history's death
And strewn like paper flowers
Upon the lotus feet of perfect masters
Saints and harlots, vagrant
Leaders, and dying kings

      This is us—
      As we are

      A race of tyrants
And we will always slay each other
If out of the darkness we come blind
And unwilling, lost in crowds of heroes
Painted with stories past and secrets held
      From beginning to end

Cycles

The wave of youth
The energy of decay and growth
Will always collapse and expand
Roll inwards and break
      Upon alien shores
And above all else—gather low
In the sunken places of the earth
To expand our collective limbs
However subversive
And dig them rebellious
Into the veins of an ugly god

One culture, stacked high upon
      Every inch of itself
One and together time throughout
Broken staggered blood, submerged
      Beneath the ideals
Of too many generations in agreement
Dancing awkward in the same directions
Armed with the same tools
Forging idols from the same mold
To stand boldly upon each other's shoulders
And face an onslaught of the elders

Gathering our instruments aflame
And expanding consciousness
Beyond the pale light of commonality
To see at once forward and deep
Into our today and a tomorrow undreamed

Except by all those who came before us
In different words and ways
We always sing the same troubles
        To a different tune
Riding the crest high
So sure we should never again
Face the weakness of aging
And the question—what should we do?

Perhaps one day, we will reach
Across the ages and dance together
In a ritual fire

Perhaps, in time we will see through time
And no more shall we climb the summit
To the feet of a dark evening tomb
Holding hands steady as we enter weary
Into shared spaces of gathering shame
        And shelter

        If for only once
Fear would not drive us on
To act out the same tired plays
The same endless cycles
Of minds on a one-way street
And cultures fixed like trams
In determinate grooves

If only we could dream of something real
And stay silent and strong

And be transformed truly
Inwardly for the only revolution

Perhaps then the wave
Would cease to break
And flow mighty into a river unyielding
Gathering in unison like reeds
At the mouth of our only source

An Impossible Task

With every whim and word
I drop heedless upon the page, unending
I set for myself an impossible task
A journey wide across
The ocean of humanity
Dreaming for something
We cannot put into words

Lucky for me
I long ago dropped the notion
That either my heart or words
Were going anywhere

That a result was something real
And that winter
Turned into spring
Like an apparatus upon a spoke
Eternal rotation around

A fading fire
Colliding rocks within space

The task of gathering
An infinite number
Of points and opinions
Voices and cries
Into a single song
To combine the energy
Of ten thousand suns
Into a paper frame

How necessary it has become to do so
To contain the multitudes
Within a series of glances
However brief and impartial
They may be

For although the world
Will never listen
Perhaps, if we unite
Enough of the screaming
Into a marching wind
The impossible task
May also see the truth—
That greatness is a matter
Of all things small
And that one time
Together, all at once
Can transform this heaven earth

And send a tremor of calm deep
Into the collective insanity

I know this muddy road of mine
  Is going nowhere
  Except in circles

Yet lucky for me
I long ago abandoned the notion
That power and change
Were at the end
Of a long and dreary path
And not hidden
Like a gem that shines
Even in the mud
Coming and going, ceaselessly
With hands held down
In the first and last steps
  Of the end

The Burning Wheel

  Screaming fire sun
  Misty morning rain
Sets silent and calm over the mountain
  I have become

A bird calls into the distant emptiness
Showing me once and again
That all silence is mystical

And that the womb of matter
Is a stark and pregnant emptiness
Full to the frayed brim
Bursting with form and pattern

Here at the edge
Of a tattered precipice
Is the abyss—staring back at me
Reflecting the world in full glory
Turning from the wooden rim of one spoke
Through each of the seven planes

And each is on fire
With the greed and infatuation
Of a people burning
From the inside out

Life goes eternal, on and on
For a thousand patient lifetimes
And the wheel keeps on turning itself
One spin at a time, burning
And drifting like a flower in the mountain breeze
Petals wafting lazy upon the shadowed earth

Oakland

People of a forgotten town
Deserted in knowledge
Halfway between two ideal extremes
The middle way for weirdoes and losers

Where old blood flows in murky rivers
Down broken street corners
Sunken ever so slightly
Into the battered skin of a concrete park

Where confused youth
Come to end their confusion
And wander aimless through a familiar scene
The middle way of an endless cultural change
      Serene and quiet
      Yet full to capacity
With all that goes unmentioned between us

Chattering beggars amass
With outstretched hats and hearts and hands
Free of the overflowing crazy spit
Of that towering hipster jungle
A little further out west

A refuge for all those not quite strange enough
To be anything but in between times
Waiting to grow up, waiting for something
      And in the meantime
      Joining hands triumphant
      Across the kickball field

Where we paint on all the wrong walls
Never finding ourselves until the last minute
And houses sit comfortable and multicolored
Like a sunny hillside
In an unknown Greece

A strange desperation beneath the seaside air
A feeling you cannot pin down
A sneaking suspicion that you are surrounded
On all sides by vagrants and thieves
Friends and old acquaintances
All at once, breathing
An unknown fear that chains us
In a stationary stampede
Of working class bums and white hills
With eyes that see only wealth

Land of friendship and liquor shops
Where walking down the dim lit street
Is a matter of common faces and sly smiles
And that mumbling guy around the avenue
Markets and gritty holes in the wall
Mom and pop shop from a country
      Of unknown origin

Where lakes are man made
And gondolas drift lazy through
Trash and shit and fairyland
And people walk sideways
And ride scraper bikes
Into all hours of the night
Seeking something unknown
Lost in the great divide

Split into a careful three
Down the tracks and murder docks
Where giant cranes hover

Like fossilized lizard beasts
Dinosaurs of the Bay
Raiders of a western Detroit
A port for the entire world
Where industry faded long ago
Into scrap iron warehouses
And abandoned train yards

Where artist and sculptors lay low
And sprout between the tattooed cracks
And music flows into a sea of dingy bars
Where the underground is above
And we sing together drunk about the nothing day

Middle city that history forgot
Where time split wide and left behind
The dreams of so many unwanted youth
Where language faults and morphs
And the mother tongue of generations
Is an ebonic kaleidoscope of shifting words
And meaningless gestures
Needy and overeager

        Oakland
Dirty and grimy
Dusty and flowered pocket
Of friendship and tall cans
Hipster halfway house
Of the meandering generation
We will find our way through the shithouse
World of garbage dumped in our sweaty laps

And together take that stick
And wade through the oldest blood
As a united and proud
Drunk, belligerent, and unwieldy tribe
A shining jewel in the eastern bay

Silent Strong

And again, I will remain silent
And bear with gentle good humor
The weight of other people's insanity
Through the nonsense, I will come strong
And do my best to make sense
Out of a rambling story
Told in fragments
From the barren middle
Like I always have

I will carry the weight you give me
But I will not return the favor
I will again be a light unto myself
An example of the simple act
You could never grasp
Of letting oneself go
Despite your delusions

For all the years you dumped your garbage
        In my world
For all the years I remained silent
I have remained alone and strong

But now, after all the gifts of anger given to me
And all the years of solitude
      It is not enough

And just in time, here she comes
To ruin or save my world
And show me a clear picture
Of the end of my life
And all the love I truly need

Amores (IV)

Intoxicated again by the light of your very presence
I stumble wide eyed and wanting through my fuzzy world
A klutzy mess of useless reasoning and doubt
Still terrible at this meandering single life

Every tiny event, every bizarre step of life and love
Reveals to me who and what and all that I am—noisy
And ready, ready for the doubts to end
With the long and sleepless nights

So here we are together with only walls and glass
A mountain of difficult words between us
And I am a puppy lost in our undefined energy

Silly and stupid and wandering in my mind
Through silky fields of golden hair and ivory thighs
Dreaming and dreaming and dreaming of you

A Song for the Rain

Light reflected hopeful through
The evening trees
A rain drifts in a flickering slant
Between falling sun leaves
And tiled rooftops, ascending
Into the bright and lazy clouds
Of a summer day wasted
In fog and lightning

As wheels fade sharp
And directionless
Into a distant road
And the secret lives of others
Wade on and on in cadence
The full sky opens itself
Heavy and gray
And love beats cold
For us to drink from within

Friendships perhaps
Are no more
What they once were
And never again do our
Troubled days sing in longing
For all that we waste
Between wood and hours
And all the rippling regret
That drifts behind us

Quiet rooms that spread
Empty into the arms of night
Shadow and silence
And doors closed shut
Between lost moments
Past and a hollow embrace
Shifting from
An old memory
To a now ignored

And still here through all
The shifting sadness and peace
The rain persists joyful
In its own wishful song
And morning reveals
An ice from the crying sky
And me still sitting somewhere
Between a yes and a no

How many pass the day
Behind doors shut long ago
With steam in the air
Flickering screens
And pages open to wherever
Staring out of windows
At the branches swaying
As if trying to tell us something
We already knew

A quiet hum sinks
Into the back of minds

And together we know
That somewhere, someone
Is singing the same song
And smiling softy
In the corner of the mouth
As the rain beats and hail falls
Into all our careful plans

Born in Debt

Going the long, untaken road
Back home to a gritty picture
Taken before I was ever born
I stand starry eyed and loved
       Cradled in the arms
Of debt collectors and the oiled gears
       Of a turning machine
Wheels grinding me away, slowly
Into the negative plane

A gift I received indirectly
Shaping my bones and nerves
Into a vessel ready to receive
The human game of chance
And through the chaos
Of shouting and stand offs
A picture was painted for me
A picture of cause and effect
A picture out of another's past
A picture of people on the bottom rung

Out of luck and time
And in the middle
Was me without a clue or a chance
Or any say in the matter

But I was the gleam in the eye
And the responsibility
For getting into this mess
Was my own
It was a far out gamble
A cosmic masochism
Of my own design

But regardless of fault and failure
I walk through a troubled world
Free of blame and regret
For no amount of symbols in place
Of what is felt and real
Could move me from my foundation
Of clay, soil, and root
Spreading universal into a thousand
Corners of the human heart

We, my blood and chain
Will make it to an end
Of some fashion and as always
It will be of our own making
And it shall sit unmoving in a whirlpool
Like a candle's flame
A stream of elegance and decision
A fitting construction

Of lives lived in fits of darkness
And narrow shafts of light

For if there is anything at all that I am
It is deserving and devious, behind
The play, the drama, the act
      Of my simple life

Like many of my day and time
I was not born
With a silver spoon
But rather an iron noose
And with my head held unflinching
In the lies and nonsense
Painted in pictures long before I was born
I run the long way home

An Elegy in Three

I found you lying
Dead beside the road
Another life cut short
A tragic omen, whispering
Pale and drained of the magic
And frisk of wagging tails
And the eager yelp
A companion now
For no one, a sign
Eviscerated under gray skies
Sending fearful waves of horror

And shock through the fragile
Body of the world

What strange vision are you?
What am I even to feel?

Not but a quiet day
Before a dear light
Was extinguished
Like a leaf of grass in the wind
Of a traveler's dream

Dear friend out there
Lost in the world
I mourn for more
Than what we have suddenly lost
For as another soul, too young
Ascends inwards to truth
To the other side of life

With him another tiny beacon
Has flickered out
In the endless dark

Perhaps, I am selfish
To mourn for what is lost
To want in desperation
To hold close and keep
Something so fragile for myself
To preserve a falling flake of snow
As if it could last forever

Perhaps, I should have known
That decaying vision so briefly seen
And passed by was a sign
And I should have warned the world
Of something I could not have know

And so now, in the midst
Of your adventure
You are pulled back into sadness
And for this I am sorry
And I know it is hard
To see meaning and reason
In something so tragic as this
As if either existed
Beyond the human heart
Perhaps they do
But for us with eyes
So small and so young
      We cannot see
And in shaking love
We shall join hands and sing low
For him and all he would have been
      And done

My part as always is small
And unknown, and my story
Will sputter along behind the scenes
No one need mourn
For the little things I lose
For it seems that I am not destined
For anything that I desire

But only to lose everything
Slowly until all I have
Is emptiness

If only I could lose
My longing, my desires, my yearning
Along with everything else
Maybe then in the wake of tragedy
I could think beyond
My own confusing needs
That even now
The only thing that I want
Is to be with her
And embrace in warmth
All those tender things
We are supposed to live and die for

I hope that one day
I will have an answer
As to why I am always alone
            But I do not
And for now, I will sit quiet for you
And keep the fires of wonder
From burning out in the endless dark

And I will mourn for three
For you, our dear friend
For a gift I believed might have blossomed
And for a dead puppy, once loved
On the side of the road

As You Are

You—the heart and the pure air
The light of the morning calm
The best of me in smiles
Always an embrace beyond
What is possible and could be for us
A starlit dream electric
And a power from within
For throughout the world of will and union

    Is you—
    As you are

In a vision of closeness and soft skin
A collected photograph in every color
In a hanging eye of moon shade and blue
Centered steady in sweetness and light
The mind calling me to lonely hands
And your scent caressing me into a lull
Where I am nothing but falling
Down into a hole beneath your breast

An old flag bearing times past and shown
You as always come in waves
Like an ocean in the night lake
Sailing against the wind of my shame
    Taking many shifting
Forms in a steady concept I create
Projecting a likeness of why and who
You could be and so many things

Except perhaps the thing you are
Which is everything but mine
And just a little beyond
In the open canyon wound
Of forlorn moss
But I could never dream
Of having you if that meant
Keeping you in a cage
As a bird without song
And I would never be happy
If you were anything but free
      Even from me
And my simple wishes
For I love you as nothing more
Than what you are

      As you are

But as the flowers drift silent and soft
Through the twilight daze
I will remain smiling for you alone
With all of you rushing into me
A welcome possibility of the new
Held tight in hands unsure
And cherished even if only
You were mine in a daydream
Too far from being unworthy
In the opinions of the cynical
Who know so few facts
Of my inside room

So please go
And remember that of all those
You meet and all the happy fools
Who fall in love with you
That I see and accept you
As you are

Expulsion

Tongue strip bare
Forest of the pounding heart
Lush pure secret
Kept in expulsion
Knees unfolding down
Squeeze shut mind
Towering fingers of ivory
The ache of years
Within the house
Of sweat and breath
Show me tightness and silk
Welling forth from me
Lashes flutter stare
Deep together
Hills in one rhythm
And all the lips swell
And bring me in
To reach you till you're bare
And soft and sweet
So I may give myself
And intertwine the long

Center searching
For the middle
Of this moment song
Gentle moon pool eye
Staring back strong
And whisper me down
To your heaven smell
Drip skin warmth
And tongue strip bare
Forest of our pounding heart

Unrequited

How could I presume
That one such as you
Might begin to accept
But a little of the loneliness?
An open wound that could never bleed
In someone as lovely and magnetic as you

A gash forever receding
Into early beginnings
Heartbroken from the cradle
The dawn of a lonely wreck
And the honest order
A pain intimate and draining
For as long as we have walked friend
Side by side through this diverging story
I have slunk in the dim shadow
And you in the exalted light

For all the tearless ones
Who share with me a
Heartache bereft and stabbing
Unknown to the lucky
This towering wall
Of unwarranted hardship
The one-sided beating in the chest
This, friend, is our sacred
Space for us alone

And for all who are blessed
Not to fall into vicious circles
      Of love unrequited
I sing so you may see us clearly
      And forgive us
For never learning how to be like you
And so, you may then see for our sake
How easy you have it
In our wanton gaze

How does it feel to stare
For years into distant judging eyes?
With so much bursting potential
      And so much passion
      Stunted and unused
      And so, propelled
      In all the hidden directions
Surfacing in the poorest of times
To shoot ourselves in the foot

How do we drag ourselves along?
When each time we gather together
Our integrity and build a gift
To grant hopeful to another
That gift is spat upon
And trampled under foot
Like so much wrapping paper
In an ungrateful wind

A riddle wrapped in a mystery
The big unanswered question
Of the endless quest
How by the grace of fairness
And balance interchanged
Does the universe falter so often
And work against so man
From our myopic view?

      And in turn
How do so many with so little
Stumble so easily into the garden
Of togetherness and touch
And mistreat, neglect, and abuse
The wonders which they take for granted?

How does it feel to watch
As the careless disregard
And prattle on in laughter?
Stuffing themselves fat
In front of a starving child

As the list of faces and names grows
Ridiculous to the point of absurdity
I cannot help but spout
A waterfall of tired words
In an attempt to describe something
Even resembling the truth
Of who and what I am
And why in this oddity
   Of a planet
I cannot find something so simple
   As a companion
With whom to share my potential

And for all of you who understand
What it means to give your heart freely
To another and remain innocent
As they turn their backs on you
To retain hope and not become
A cynical joke that strides unblinking
Through honesty with a wall surrounding
And for all the lucky in whose hands
The love falls effortless
I sing so that one fateful day
We may like you be treasured as we deserve

Ignorance

Stem of darkness
Mistress of my bumbling ways
How to judge myself and life

Fair by which the roots
Of all that burden the mind
Come pouring out
The unconscious depths

Energy clogging action
Obvious in hindsight
Clouded sensations
How to see the clear day
Through inner fog
And clarify the ore
Of the human make
Binding us, spine and cell,
To forms fully human
And in need of sustenance
In both body and mind

Surely, I am an idiot for thinking my life
Free from conditioning influence
That freedom itself was something owed
And deserved by a mere process of time
That in time, the web of life
Would untangle and the reasons
I make myself miserable would raise
Like roses from a decomposed stem
And all would click logically into place

I know more than well
Who I am and the eternal
Rotating cave behind my eyes

Is a spring always renewing if only
I could base my life from there

I know that what I am
Is also what you are
And we are That
Yet as the vision wells up
From my old bag of meaning and faith
I cannot help but to widen my eyes
In awe and gasp at my own foolishness

For again and again, I find
It is so simple and obvious
Yet never in all my dreaming
Do I wake up to any
Of these things which I profess
To be true and easy and sound
For words are but a sketch
Drafted by us who are like
A dumb soul who has had
The most beautiful of dreams

Anchor of darkness
You are shared by the act of birth
Among all us fevered searchers
Acting by whims of the stomach
Trying to eat our words and numbers
Guided by magnets below the belly

But I do not worry about awakening
For although you pervade me

And I am held shear by the pillars of suffering
I am light and know with ease that you
Are only a mirage, and one does not
Go around hitting at mirages with a stick

Craving

The bitter sting
The cold biting cringe of
A bird caged
In the constricted chest
A wraith floating endless behind
We who clutch and cling to life
Desperation, a phantom want
Filling this bottomless hole within
And through this iniquity
Becoming a completed picture
Somehow made whole by the addition
Useless layers to an imagined self

The wave of reaction climbs
Up and down
The experience of life offered
Both sought and unsought
Flows, and
In this wave sits a noble truth
That the more we feel pleasure
The more vulnerable we are to pain
And whether burning in foreground
Or background, the pain

Is always with us
Biting at the back of our heels

So, it becomes easy to want and receive
To welcome pain with open arms
Into the harem walls of the crest, to feel
And let yourself slide deep
And warm into blissful sleep
Overcome with joy and lust
The happy thirst which knows
That water must soon be coming
To break free of the pressure
And let the positive energy overflow
The selfish senses

But what happens when it all disappears?
When in the wake of the positive
Breaks the wave and comes the minus
Side of human sensation?
And what was once joyful and easy
Dissolves and sitting noble
In your heart and mind
Is the other side of pleasure?

For perhaps the worst pain of all is loss
To look back and feel an apparition
Of something pure you once had
And reach with quaking hands backward
To grasp and pull yourself once again
Into the lighter side of things, the preferred side
If only you could feel that way again

To be young or smiling in the heights of love
If only it did not have to leave us

For maybe, it is the preference
The seeking and groping blind
The crushing of life
Like a butterfly in the palm
Tight and unable to fly with the wind

If only we could see the scale, the wave
That comes and goes, hot and cold as always
And that beyond the craving, the phantom want
      Is a still peace untouched

Aversion

From all outward appearance
A spark, an interval between one
Eternal darkness and another
A life so brief and full of color
Confronted with so much to understand
And so frail a form by which to carry
Around an unsubstantial state

The earth from out of which we grow
Bathed in light and warmth and air
Brings forth from itself
Strange and wonderful
Creatures, yet none so strange
As we who go mumbling along

Trying to understand, trying to poke
Our intellects into fire and rain
Mashing our fingers into places
      We do not belong

Because perhaps together
We may one day create a world free
From all this dreadful pain and hunger
From poverty and sickness
And we may go on living forever
As dreadful skeletons bereft of mystery
No longer subject to deal
With all this uncomfortable life
If only we could just cure the cancer
And then cure once and for all
This disease called death

For isn't that what we really want?
Why we rush around like mad
Gathering up our wealth into solitary piles
So we may rage angry against it—
The great and terrifying end

For how many of us hurry through life
Wincing at scraped knees
And gobbling down medicine?
How many of us resort
To a prescription answer?
And why for so long
Have we waged war in futility
Against our own fundamental truth?

Ignorance and fear
Confound the understanding
In a failure to see that as we push
And avert our attention
Away from the bite of pain
And bury our heads in the sand
That pain can only grow and become
Large, full of power and validity

Sinking into a cramped
And claustrophobic mind
Jumping at shadows and creaks
In the distant imagination
Is we who cannot relax in the middle
Of what we dare not admit
And let what has arisen fall back to its source
Where all is impermanent
Like a stream of fire

Surely there are none as strange as we
Who fear death

The Lotus Land

Even now beyond the limits
There extends a passage way
Beyond the prison of our gated knowledge
Spiraling forever outward
From the shared center mind
Like gold it shines even in the furnace

And radiates like a million rays
From the mouth of a one pointed sun

    Going or returning
Remaining forever unmoved
Abiding within the particulars, now
Every action, every event and challenge
Becomes a Buddhist's work
And across a sea of twisting impressions
Unwinding in the deep soul dissolved
We float upwards into the flowered air
Sitting on jewels of mud

Living compassion in realization that
This very body is the Buddha
And this earth the lotus land of purity

Through all the movement and chaos
Striding tranquil and unattached
Are those who take themselves lightly
And so go dancing beyond the ground
Flying wingless with angels before death
Living examples of our human destiny
As keepers of wisdom and love
    In this universal bridge

Intoxicated

Alone by the garnet glow
Of the long desert night

I follow a trail of tears dreaming
Of the countless times I have felt
The bare touch of your garment
And the caress of your hand
Firmly resting in mine
And so often have I cried out thirsty
For the scent of your sweet nectar
Only to open my eyes blurry
And discover in amazement
The weight and grace
Of my own weak hand
And the soft alight
Of my own tattered clothes
Pressed upon the skin of this
Old world wanderer
Intoxicated staring intent
At the fact of my being weighed
Down head to foot in desires
Made a slave by the chattering
Heart and mind knowing that
I should be god in reality
Where my spirit is desireless
From ascending death by death
       Why should I fear?
When have I ever been less by dying?
Let me be what no mind ever conceived
And sacrifice my angel soul
So I may wander drunk about the tavern
And bring you good tidings
From the hidden world
Open the folds of your veil

And you shall find no barrier
Between lover and beloved
And all manifestation latent therein
Shall remain oblivious to what comes
In and passes out of the mind
Leaving the petals of a rose scattered
About the dusty floor seeking
From door to door I go
By night under a crescent moon and
Out from the same entrance
      From in I came
Following the musical notes
      Only to find one
Eternal sound prevailing
From the echoing trail
Of caravans in the distance
How should I reveal to you?
That in my intoxicated daze
Of the bliss we imbibe therefrom
Your face is reflected in my cup
Of dirty common wine
And that by the light
Of the rose-colored sun
I come to you longing
Oh, August Master!
Lead me by the hand
As I traverse the path on foot
As you ride effortless along it
To the high house
Atop the tallest palm

From where I fell
And broke my neck singing

To you we shall return!

Amores (V)

Now intensified so in the wake of my acceptance
By you I long ever the more and swell at the incessant
Thought of your charm and fullness, the curve
Of your yielding lips and the scent of you calling me home

I know now that I can live content with loving someone
Fully and having to let them go, but I could not live
With never having loved you at all, and at least the memory
Of your touch will endure and bring me back to my faith

That I am not aimless and in fact deserve you and know
That perhaps you might desire me too if only circumstance
And poor timing was the sad folly of someone else

And I thank you for being honest and true to yourself
For it is not some concept, some idea that I love
But you and maybe one day fate will call us home

As One Is

Here, standing at the ragged edge
I look out calm and collected

Over the world's supple and curving form
And celebrate the release of all this
Meaning and direction
That once belonged to me
And everything I assume
I give to you freely if only
So you may share yourself
With me and laze about
Maskless and naked in the wild night

For now, I will be like rabbit
And descend from the corner
Of a distant belt of stars and
With my words loosened and soundless
I shall gather up the pieces of our hardship
And offer you a messy bushel
Of uncarved stone and unbleached silk
      I will presume here
       To offer you a vision
A path in the sky manifested
By which to saunter at whim
To the ends of heartache or even
To a joyous end of the frantic search
For some collection of polished beads
And gadgets of electric light
By which to define us rightly and full

I shake my fists and pound a skinless drum
And laugh at my own misdoings and
From the top of a dune of sand and pebbles
I roll like one who has tripped

Over his own square feet
And at the base of perfection found
A gentle kiss to share wet and warm
Breathing with you alone and yes
To run through fields of verdant life
And embrace you tight with the skinny arms
That fall hapless by my aching sides

I sound myself, and I am heard
Through endless miles of deserted wood
And the feeling of being alone in a crowd
Gives way to knowing that I am the crowd
And that I am the deepest desire
Of the earth that dare not set itself free
And the patient cries of a people
Demanding change, a growth
   Never seen here before

And turning, dazzled and amused
I confront you with a dizzy of questions
And answers beguiled and
Demanded of all us lost children
Dazed and confused in the grownup jungle

Have you ever been to your own silent depths?
Have you followed the narrow road to the end of thought?

And come to a place where feeling
Is not separate from imagination?
How long have you lived in a daydream? And
Where do you begin and end?

Feel with me your edges and limits
As if they were tangible and not
A border held in common
With the universal ground

Who is it that carries this corpse around?
For I hear talking all around me
And nothing heard is either sensible
Or telling of a truth found in the inner eyes
Common sense being the most uncommon accident
And nonsense the acidic mother tongue
Of crowds and miseducated sirens

I poke and prod and tickle the very center
Of your unfelt lie, your belly of molted armor
Your long flowing enigma
And I know that you know
That you are not you and neither am I
Although you don't dare admit it

Have you looked into another's eyes?
And not wondered in a waiting game
Have you tasted the crumbs of another?
Only to be sure you weren't savoring
The histories of your own satisfaction

        Where are you even going?
With all these days of energy and hope
Of trying to mold your own clay morning
To an evening chiseled in the marble urge
An arrow set straight in the flightless end

Rushing too fast to see me here supportive
Standing blind beside you
For I am crude, barbaric, and unformed

I let you go from my humble bowstring
To see what you will make of wonder

For I have heard so much from the mouths
Of the young rebels and the wandering men
And the women too afraid to stop the wandering
And of all this talk I see not one small word
Getting to the heart of things

I see an army with groaning angst
Lost in their own bad news
I see a tribe of children playing as
Serious and stern as statues that walk about
I see a cosmic joke full of actors taken in
By their own fantastic drama
And a slew of comedians without enough humor
To laugh even at themselves

There has never been more creation than today
Never before has so much connection
Been sparked between the brittle nerves
Of a heaven and hell possibility
And never again will we the people
Be here now
With this expansive set of particulars
And a history yoked at the center focus
By a million uninformed decisions

And as it has always remained
Identity is as distinct as the sky and ground
And our famous words shoot upward
From the womb of matter and birth

And I see that you follow me
For your eyes are bright and shine
With the dignity of one awake and open
And no longer in wait for answers and
So grasping your familiar hand in mine
I guide you lower into the realm of yourself
And the clear and sweet scent
Of a youth dissolved in acceptance
Draws us deep into scenes from the shifting past
And a thousand gourds converge
From the mind of one knotted vine

And I run barefoot with you sure and steady
Sharing all the tethered weight
Shouldering your burdens along with you
In a sunlit ride through the phantasmal body
Of your bright inner world
And I smile as you feel ashamed
And trudge through valleys of hidden regret

And as we descend, a light
From the silver moon splinters all perceptions
And I assure you and accept you
And all that you project outward
And see as both right and wrong

And I can see you shining behind
All the careful observation and evaluations
Sown together and strung like a fabric
To cover you through a harsh winter trial
A wall to keep the world out
An illusion of safety fettering
You and all those like you
To a past life that is perhaps still being lived
A season passed in remembrance and fear
       For the changing time

What comfort is there in memory?
And what is memory other than a symbol?
A light by which to guide you through ignorance
And a falsehood built
On foundations of sand and salt

Do not worry, for as we ride
All this is left behind and
Cast off with the sickness of both the good and bad
And slowly we become light and unburdened
And all the difference between you and I
Is but a stupid notion laughed about in jest

And as always, I whisper
Soft in your receiving ear
"Come with me love"
And all around us are signs and wonders
And the earth dream rushes up to meet us
Bringing with it the good news

And weathered pilgrims from the whale's belly
With rough bare feet and matted hair

And the smell of decay that follows
Is not a problem for through this offering
We see the fullness of life worth living
Only to remark and lilt and laugh
At the profound fact that the strangers
Walking about the twilight calm
Are in fact alive and not dead
And so a simple nod becomes so much more
And the masks of god shift about
If only they could agree with each other
For but a brief second in this raging squall

For as you reflect yourself in the light
Of my watchfire embers
I come piercing through a fog
And clear and sharp is my diamond soul
If perhaps a little clouded for
Having too much less and not enough
More in this lifetime than anyone should bear
And yet still strong enough
To have never lost myself in the lack
And the unseen judgment behind
The screen of our passing whims

And journeying takes us beyond definitions
Where a picture of life becomes real and actual
And together after all our beliefs are stretched thin
And have died and passed on

To where we do not know
A truth comes riding a winged horse
Upon a cloud striped flame
Reciting an ongoing story
Of the human creed

A tale of nothing but our own doing, how we are
And a knowledge that freedom is found
As one is and not as one should be

And we breathe deep the offered air
Honest and plentiful and headstrong
Dancing along the pathless land
Going nowhere in particular
And loving every inch of beauty now
Before it withers and hardens
      As all things do
Like a willow's branch
After the winter fall

And I too wither before you for
Although I recite a halfwit song of garbled meaning
I am unaware of my own truth and so unaware that
I too am not made by either beliefs or dreams
Events, occurrences, or the mercy of others
For those arise still and pass away into obscurity
I am not a stagnant pool of water or a hidden oasis
But a river swirling onwards into the great ocean
I am not an idea in your mind fixed and unchanging
But the creation of all you need personified here

For you alone in the light of rebirth
And a revolution profound and within

I am not an island or a universe or part of one
I am not my words or my voice
      For neither belong to me
Because I did not make them—the world made them
And my mind and heart too have become lost
Carried away by the frozen river of sight

      For I am not original
I am only a trickster who has read too much
And thought far too much for my own good
And so let my intuitions fall
By the wayside in a display of vulgarity
And encouraged self-destruction

I am the product of an era mesmerized and
Enchanted by a flickering box
And my thoughts are but a recording
Of all the teachers who came before me
Of those who were just as stupid and daring as I
A series of gramophone records repeating
Wisdom from out the crystal past

I cannot create your happiness
I cannot import anything from the outside
I can only see a shadow cast
As if it were already there
And implicit within you
Not something elusive and mystic

But a fact of life in the greenroom
Just behind the stage

And here at the end of the world's light
At the final stretch of our journey
Together in perpetual circles
Going nowhere except headlong
      Into the mouth
Of the same familiar place
From whence we started
Realizing now that there are two ways back home
One to run the long road 'round the world
Through darkened cities and rusted shrines
The other to stay put and know well
That home is here and that all places
      Are the same place

Looking deep into the liquid blue
Of your gentle and forgiving eyes
I am confounded and questionless
And none of my words can explain
Even a fraction of what is before us
And even less of what is behind us
And reality as it seems is unimportant
And irrelevant as a mere concept
And what truly matters is not what was
But what is and we cannot change that
No matter how hard we try, and we do try
And so as I watch you pass the night in dream
I can see you still departed

Still in some afternoon long gone
In their idealized arms

So, I depart with the air and cloud

I let you go as I know I must and
I kiss you long and deep and hold you tight
As if for a thousand unwearying autumns
I traverse your snow covered thighs
And night and day are given over to pleasure
And although it will not last
I rest in your strength and generosity
For I know that nothing happens to you by chance

At morning there are peach boughs hanging
Over the barred gate beyond the bridge-rail
And out past the horizon I hear the song of birds
And watch the sunrise through the clear dawn
Cherishing you and this gift of your company

You will hardly know me before I am gone
And perhaps one day far from now
When we are both ready
And life itself has let me in to its selective garden
I will at last meet the real you
In a foreign land where dreams
Become a fertile and living thing
And not a sorrow falling like rain
Over the jet black sea

And again at the end of all my searching
I find myself where I have always been
Alone, untamed, and burnt by the desert sun
      Adrift on an endless river
Just reflecting the sky's tinge
In a boat full of jesters, beggars, and fools
Wandering musicians with jeweled flutes
And wine rich for a thousand glasses
I hang my head the same old way over the railing
And collecting the scattered pieces of my life
I ascend inward to swim in my belt of distant stars

I will not forget you or the way you held me however brief
And for as long as I go dancing about this earth
I will remain yours and be here now, as I am, as one is.

Part IV
Tears of the Desert
101 Poems

2009-2011

...THE SOUND OF the rain needs no translation...

I

Always, I find you here
The years twist and turn; still, it remains the same
The change lingers beyond the light of these tired eyes
I am always yours and will not forget

The swelling lightness in your chest
The way you look in the morning
The heavy, lingering feeling of a time you're holding on to
I look upon you through your own eyes

Behind the smile, I know you feel the same
In the darkness of dreams, we are united, and
All the yesterday dissolves, lost in clouds of red and white

Together we are the earth, the moon,
And the space between; in you, I am lost
It bursts and devours the place we once shared

II

Have I lost you? Dancing one
Your face always changes
And tills the soil of new laughter
What is not lost can never be found

Clinging to what I have not had
You come alive in a vision of clouded tears
Through you, I am whole
In you, I see my origin and the source of my changing ways

The fires of now consume the clenching fists,
And you are revealed in nakedness and lonely eyes
The sky opens in your smile as you walk away

You are the center and axis of a dying world
A flower turning in the wind
A glance is all the hope I need

III

Blue, piercing stare
Autumn leaves and scarlet hair
Wandering, you never know what you want
Behind you are the footsteps of my youth

We are the adventure into the wilderness of a darkened
age
The voices too loud to hear
I see myself reflected in a thousand screams; uncertain,
Beautiful, magnificent, embracing the emptiness beneath

Hardened by years of quiet passion
The sun, blood and time
Ended in an instant, forgotten in the blue and piercing
stare

Wide and awake, longing, lost, wanting
Together, we voice the last words ever spoken
      And bury ourselves in autumn leaves

IV

A light that dwells in the depth of darkness
Seeking the end of all things sprung from emptiness
The desert beyond language, beyond the limits of the heart
The mind stops by a love that moves in shadow and sleep

Onward, the pilgrim walks, the whale and the ivy
We flow together in the belly of a paradox, and
The lonely giant stirs in the hidden corners
Always, we wonder, and always, we fear

      In you, we are naked and incomplete
      Your silence is louder than we can hear
Thunderous silence, and the universe burns in fire

Śiva only dances, and all things end at the center
All things spiral out from there; It flowers forth and returns
For that center you, and to you we shall return

V

Crashing shores, twisting tunnels of wind
Deserted, wandering from dream to dream

Looking back, I see the waves of a distant ocean
In you, I lost myself; alone, I sing your song

Your grace is my strength, your body—my soul and hands
Seeking the tender caress of blind and longing eyes
    Too far—the way back from here
    Madness—the only promise of men and fools

    Sometimes naked,
Here they roam the desert isle
I am you, my long-lost friend

How beautiful your song; how lovely your hidden face
    The end of all that never began
    It is always you and forever it is lost

VI

    Welling up from starry black
It pours over the heart, drowning the mystery
    It was always you, little one
Turning and smiling in the wandering night

My heart revolves on the world's edge
In secret, you speak of promises and broken thoughts
It was you on the night's breeze and in the passing trains
Running from me in my own embrace

The flame is still alive
The black has receded in shadow and ruined vanity
The light wraps you in strength

It should be me; it always was, yet never is
For so long, I learned to be silent, and in every
Moment, I am the golden roar that deafens your world

VII

Crashing through my supple world
Again, you come to the foot of silent despair, what
Did you lose that awful night? Why did you bring your
Fire to me, only to quench it in the coolness of another?

What thankful mirror showed you where I lived?
Stranded in the innocent house of dreaming days
You found in me a strange and bitter hope
And I know, you could not let it go

In you, I found the heights of something unreal, false,
Destructive; you took from me the shell and the child
And brought me into clear and open wilderness

Through rose colored flesh and gentle touch
In candlelight, we shook the earth and tore down the sky
I am waiting for the day we aren't waiting anymore

VIII

Night sky moves sideways under laughter and fading
hands
We knew it then—the secret no one can live
Giving in to the sweetness of a living heart
The river flowed mighty and onward with the going water

Night gave way to softness and curves; eyes squeezed shut
and throbbed like an open flower, collapsing under years
of wasted fantasy—the notion of an ideal loss
    No more thinking, no more

    You showed me I was not lost
    Release and sigh with me
The mountain and the waking breath

    If only you were not one
    But you were enough
And I was born again, the owner of my own ideal loss

IX

My deepest roots, still growing, always a part of me
Knots intertwine amidst a sea of purple and the deepest
Cloud, always receding, always escaping my grasp
Never to be pinned down

You come and go, and sometimes I see you; sometimes,
I only see myself; water slips through clutching hands

Debris and ash blur my present vision
    You are not the same

    Where are we now?
Hips move in gray and subtle lines
Outwardly, we play the tragedy

Clothed in fact, our truth is strangled
In your hands, it moves free and uninhibited
You are my greatest faults in living form

X

Once, we were more than nothing; for years,
You danced in the mirror of my eye, through rain and
Falling night, through wind that breathes in friendship; in
Symbol and dream, you are the knife that tears my wings

For what could have been and for all that was
I never could let go of your eyes and the way you walked
behind him; never an inch of your flowing lips,
And still, you shine through the sleeping sea

    You will not find me in your past
It was too much for my strength to bear, but always,
Your fire will burn in the depths of my existence

The wound returns without your guidance, the well
And the shadow are wrought with the promise of another
Guiding me to the shining shore of another world

XI

Here they appear on earth
In the eye of the fool, not all men are free
The wall crumbles under its own weight
And here sits a young man in nakedness and poverty

In your reflection, all things become clear and void
In sight, all things become separate and distinct
Union is blurred by the very act of perception
Buried under a tangled mess of names and false tongues

Laughter in the distant night and bells in the silent shade
I turned up a stone and found you underneath
But your name was faded and broken like my own

Speak and no one hears; dance and no one moves
I died, and no one is dead
For here they appear on earth

XII

Walking in familiar places
I found something I thought was lost
It was hidden in plain sight
Among the trees, the light, and the turning world

Falling in love with the center of everything, the deepest
Inmost skin, clothed in outsides and smiling faces, the
rotating night, the dome of the universe melting under my
feet; I am not even sure I am anything

Eyes wide open
How wonderful it is that no-thing is the same
And that everything appearing to be is not so

Once again, I have been fooled
The child moves freely in the garden
Surrounded by bees and growing vines

XIII

Fasting the heart
The wind is walking on me
The mind becomes clear, buoyant
Revealing the universal center

Vast emptiness, nothing holy
Lost in the deep forest above the sun
Beyond the door, it expands and passes away
Ritual fires of abandonment consume the creator

Coming and going, ceaseless, no movement
Deep within the self, chains are breaking and floating
Upwards, groping in the dark womb of our great mother

Rising, falling, spiraling inward
The actor turns to leave the stage
A drop dissolves in the endless ocean of you

XIV

Remembering you with hands clenched
For that moment, we saw each other, boundless
    Eye to eye in the burning sun
My soul's desire, embodied in a forbidden atlas of curves

Dusty freckles, dreaming in your smile
I knew you long before the day we were doomed
Stolen by the shadow from my broken hands
For years, I watched you fall with grace and innocence

You are the greatest love I never had
My greatest questions unanswered
We would have been magnificent

Dreaming gives way to empty beds and open doors
The heart moves in curious ways
Damn the cruel love that flows in this world

XV

Days roll backwards; memories live and die
In the silent space between hope and joy
Light flashes and pierces the running mind
In an instant, you embrace the solitude

Drunk with softness and a gentle scent
You race wild before closing eyes

And fade again with the light of now
Kissing and singing in the wind of lonely thoughts

If only you were not despair
A bitter dream on longing lips and swelling skin
The reflection in a dying eye

Who is it that writes your name across the future?
In every step, I feel you close
For it was always me, echoing in that silent space

XVI

Like a treasure, I found you on my evening shore
Rising like smoke in rapture and decay
Even in dreams, you elude me
Always a step ahead, turning away in the radiant glow

In dreams, you are lovely and incomplete
For in life, you were just like all the others
Reaching beyond your delicate grasp
For that strange and wonderful thing I hold before you

If all the sudden
You loved me
And all the pain was yours

Please, only then may you not look for me
I have forgotten you little by little
Until that day when I could only find you in dreams

XVII

There is something comforting in this wind
Something behind the despair
The bitter cold of other human minds
It is something in the heart of the world

It speaks and whispers only when we are lost
In the low places that all humans abhor
But, that seems to be my home
With hands reaching to another shining jewel

Reflecting you just outside my grasp
Laughing at the poor fool
Beauty in the distance, always in the distance

Tonight, I cried for myself and for my old, old story
Perfect jewels in rotten hands and ugly smiles
So sure, so convinced, I only understand the change

XVIII

Even god needs a surprise
One day in the fog
I wandered off the road
And found myself in your wake

Behind me, I could hear the strange beating of my own
Footsteps, and I was sure you were a mirage

In this breaking mirror, I saw
My own present in the light of my only past

And still I am not sure you are even there
  My greatest desires
Reflected in a part of myself I haven't even met

But one day, I will find you
Because I am not much of anything
And even god needs a surprise

XIX

Standing on this shore, I can feel the smile, growing,
Lingering just beyond the corner
  All things falling into place
Today, I met a man with a golden key

For the problem of life is yet to be unlocked
There is but one answer
And only one key can open a lock—
  The right key

For years, I have stood on the ragged edge
At the doorstep of something great
Waiting for my key to roll in with the tides

Standing at the end of my world, I can feel the waves
Crashing at my feet, and with a mighty click

You fit this ancient lock, shackling me from that world
    Beyond the door

XX

I do

    Not think

        My mind

           Has ever

Known silence

XXI

The heart of the world
Is always in its people
And always in every pair of hands
Grasping and clenching
Upon the eyes of other souls

Not an inch of earth to stand on

    In the passing day, I see
The lives and dreams of sheep and wolves
Eating themselves alive in their own reflection

In solemn eyes
All forms take on the inner working
And everything fades to shadow
The marionette show
Of that once original splendor

I am the cloudy sky
That rains on my future
I am my only obstacle

The more I see of the world and its people
The more I see of myself

For as long as I cannot let myself go
You will forever remain a mystery
If I cannot see through this storm

I will forever remain
On this silent lonely shore
Broken and half a man

My end is our beginning

And we shall stand
In rapture before the misty ocean
Calm and fragrant with the flowers
Of a new and better soil

XXII

Of all the faces I wear
This may be the saddest one
The one that got lost in itself
And cannot see past this shifting desert rain

With one face, I am awake
In the other, I am absorbed in dream

     Whom do you see?
Friends, strangers, brother

I can only hope you see me for what I am
A bewildered and lonely man
A quiet child of a different time
Born with solemn eyes and a wandering heart

     I must confess
My words go one way
And my being goes another

I let the days float past me
In weakness, I see my changing face

I hear the tales of the trickster
In your voice and in mine
Laughing, with lilting eyes and a crooked smile
He says: "come off it!"

I make so many claims
If I ruined the house we built
In the name of what I left behind
For this, I am sorry

Friends, strangers, brother
I know, I am not the man you want me to be
I cannot bring you your smile
For I have lost my own

      When we meet,
I know, I bring you gifts you do not want
My burdens, my blood
And for this I am sorry

I am not yet the man I want to be
I am still the quiet child
Holding on to the toys
I found in that secret box so long ago

But in the mirror, I am smiling
And perhaps one day this little boy will laugh for real

Of all the faces I wear
This may be the saddest one
The one who found he was made of straw

XXIII

Why are you not smiling?
Were you not born today?
     You, fallen one
Victim of the oldest and closest folly

Could it be you chained yourself?
     Here you stand
And every time you move
Every time you think
You pull the chain
And bring every link along with it

     So, ask yourself
Why aren't you smiling?
     Isn't it obvious?
Is this not the only moment of your life?

The wind carries the name
Each thought remains outside you
Intertwining with the heart of a pulsing world

There has never been a moment you were not perfect
You built a house of sticks
On the foundation of the universe
And wept when it blew over in your own gale

So, who is it that sits in the sun?
     I ask so many questions
And yet none of them can rip me from my cocoon

Come back!
That is what the strings say
In the distance
You wandered out of me!

But do not fear, and please do not worry
For the way back is not far
In fact, it is too close to be seen

It is there in the breeze
Can't you hear it?
It moves when you are still
It speaks when you are silent

So then, ask yourself
Why aren't you smiling?
Were you not born today?

XXIV

If these words are truly my own
Then let them wade through
This home and devour my pity
    Only the light
    Only the cold dark waters
Shall reveal in you my eyes, my hands

Only in the word can you find freedom
Hidden in stale conversation
In passing sentences and leaking laughter

Falling from my head to the path
Made only for traveling feet

Here, I speak to my God
In my own land
I found a sword stained with the rust
Of chains and beating wings

On the wind and on the horizon
I took hold of the words
And found in them the weight of planets and suns
Buried and dying beneath the shadow
Of their only choice

They could not have known
They were losing themselves
For words were not built
To withstand such unhappiness

And yet you prevail
Beneath the skin and bitter poison

Where the road ends
You shall be my companion
Where the sun is dark
You will find me in union

If these words are truly my own
Then let me find their living vein
Let me take hold and through them

Squeeze the marrow
From the skeleton of what we say and think

So now, I will return
To speak to my own God in my own land
In blindness, in tears for the lonely desert

XXV

I find it strange
In the heights
Of great understanding
We come back
To the same dark place
Again, and again

With clear luminous heart
We shine forward
Yet still we tremble
Hesitate and grasp
At the delusions that bind us

Fabric of nothingness
In essence
Beyond grasp

All things of this life
        Move
And cannot be pinned down
Never stay still

Always changing
Always new
I too am something new
Never before and never again
      Incapable of being
An object of my own knowledge
For I cannot get out of my own skin
Grasping at smoke with illusory hands

In the light of a distant star
The corner, the hidden recess
Of inner being
Reveal themselves
      As nothing
But shadows of smoke and air
Confusions begin to surface
And the longing begins to stare

From the beginning, not a thing Is
And we are but a whispered dream
Lost among the clouded sky of reflected desire

      In the eye of self
The moon is ten thousand times and back again
      Looking down
      All above me is seen

It branches in the darkness, and
All dissolves before the light of oneness
      She is black

An unfathomable night
Washing over the pit of a loving sky

Within me
Is only you
And within you
Is only I

Where is there for revolution to take place?
Upon what does the mind stand?
Brightly, it shines nowhere
Upon nothing, does it take hold

XXVI

What a strange
Beautiful place this world is
The depths of which have no end
Born into fire
All things must be known
The mind destined
To reach the bottom of trenches
Before soaring into the sky
And dissolving
The spaces between
Darkness cannot exist
Light—a matter of presence
I cannot describe
What comes
From the corners of the soul

Insubstantial
Cannot survive
In the light of being
I was born
To see
And to know
A true nature
Through suffering
Know joy
The darkness of the human
Condition is self-created
And we share
In its momentum
If we are connected
The universe has come
To dissolve
To be shown
Truly as it is
You have more strength
Than a thousand suns
The divine lover
You will not falter
You alone bear a weight
That most could not endure
I will be like water
And surrender to all that is
Without judgment
I cannot deny what exists
It is not me
But it is there
I am stillness

And silence and strength
I am the warm center
Of a universe from where
All light shines through
I woke up one morning
From a bad dream
And found god underneath

XXVII

The new human face
With wide and helpless eyes
    We watch

The oceans bleed our cultures blood
With black and violent fervor
Our legacy of fossils

In the hands of powerful and stupid men
To crush the silent peaceful deep
In clouds of needy darkness

The life beneath the wave
The life that crawls on burning wheels
All will turn to crude and wash upon

Her stained and empty shores
Throw money at it!
    Lie and run

Circle the draining deep
Is there enough hope to fuel our racing world?
We will scream and rise

Behind the charging beast
With mind and heart
We govern ourselves

Toward a day without your oil
The ocean bleeds your bloodline
The earth is yours to lose

The human face
Will watch and weep
Our legacy in crude

XXVIII

New world
New faces
New blood
New me

Time in faded mind
Pints and tattoos
Again, and again
The challenge persists

In youth
I thought myself to be

A million thoughts
In height and splendor

But in age revealed
The low and foolish
Wisdom found
Where least expected

Growing now
Our roots in birth
Of earth and promised
Love to come

But here there
Still persists
A gnawing pale
And empty heart

That seeks and dies
In every moment
Twirling in the awkward
Light of hope and joy

     In youth
I thought myself to be
Important
To you all

But age revealed
How wrong

A child can be
When he is lied to

XXIX

Lovers left behind
Simple days
Quiet unwinding hours
Into the black rainbow
Of night and roses
Above the tide in the floating sky
Garden past the brick wall
Hanging amongst the ivy
Behind the opening gate
Beyond the mind
Closed and waiting
For the flame and the hanging wind
City of rooftops
Planet of slums
The people gave themselves
In soft and quite might
They passed away
Into the sweet and dead embrace
There we lost the dreaming
Ray of light
That shines
For always
In the deep
And silent tunnel
Past the garden

Past the gates of
The floating city
We sit in sadness
Lost in our own bad news
And regret
For the lovers
Left behind
Across the September
Stars I see
Your name
In golden clouds
And once again
We find ourselves
At the foot
Of the garden
Smiling in the crystal sun
The name is spoken
Loud it rings again
For once
We hear the song
Of the children

XXX

My closest love, let us rejoice
For we followed the flowering path
And the edge of the river
Showed us the long and winding way
Back to ourselves in the height of spring

In fear, we lost our way
In reflected burning light
Your face became my own
And I mistook you for the dawn
For here there is no darkness

Come with me, she said
Into the depths of your own silence
In trust, I will join you there
In the desert beyond language
And beyond ideas

The sky was torn, in red and silver
The mirrored waters
Shone with serene and silent brilliance
You took my hand and there
You showed my heart's only desire

In jasmine smoke
There rose in ecstasy
A hidden sign
To the land
Beyond the mountain

And together we breathed
The sweet air
Clean and pure
Forged in the dark vast pit
　　　Of our mind

In that long and lonely trek, through
Canyons of shame and fear,
Through deserts of weariness and doubt
Volcanoes of pride and
Jungles of confusion

At the center of everything
I found you laughing
And at last I knew
Who I really was

XXXI

Here in the fading light
Above the sleeping city
I come yet again
Face to face
With the silent fact

In every dark corner
At the end of every path
Down the empty corridors
I am confronted
With that strange and awful mirror

The air carries the scent
Of years and nights
And days gone past
In flight and shadowed

Breaking Open the Heart

Memories of what?
    I cannot say

And still again I cannot
Escape you in the
Dark we meet
Alone in fire
You consume the words

In frantic flight
Of mind and heart
I rush to catch you
In the open hand
That dreams of what?
      I cannot say

Yet still the hand is open
Still the mind is new
And still I cannot face
The empty
Lonely fading soul

In that mirror shines
The silent fact
Of time and still
It shouts the only truth
Of life—in you I am alone

XXXII

Life for now
Has settled down
And still my shifting world
Goes on it seems—
      Forever

Still in the back of everything
There is a ray of light
That dims and fades
And shines and moves
With sharp yet gentle strength

It lets me know
That one day the wind
Will find me unaware
Fluttered at every word
Smiling softly at the slow tick

Of that old and familiar friend—
      The clock

One day I will find it
One day the noise
Will subside and the
Turning wheels of this mind
      Will relax

And out of the mess
Out of the tangled web

Of everything that I am
Will emerge a single
      Ray of light

Perhaps one day
There will come a time
When the wheel stops turning
      But now
      Is not that time

For the sun is new every day
And my world goes on it seems forever

XXXIII

Sitting here
The streets
The snow
The trains
Go rolling past
In a flood of dreamy
Taut and swelling scenes

Of sleeping
On floors and benches
Once, at the foot
Of the world
I left to find
Something that was not lost
And could not be found

But what I remember most
Is not the people
Not the faces
Nor the endless days
Of adventure
And friendship and beer

No, what I remember most of all
Is the simple
Honest
Delight that
Saved me
Day after day

In that strange
And wonderful
Journey
At the doorstep
Of a world
I still do not know

It was you
For me
And for me alone

You go by so many names
But I shall always know you
     As surprise

XXXIV

The wind speaks of it first

That moment before everything dissolves

The language of god needs no translation

The flowers respond with a quiet nod

XXXV

The sound
The waves
The movement
The flashing of light
Shimmering and sparkling
Atop the reflection
Of my new city
My new home

Like a great symphony in motion
You opened to me
In chaos and in new life

You opened the door
  To the peace
  In all things

Looking back
To life before the tunnel
  I cling
  I grasp
At what I had
Afraid to look forward
Into that fairytale
Called the future

  But here
  On this hill
The hands and the backs
Of the people
Embrace the growing weight
Of their own tragedies
And in love and laughter
Together
We move

With one foot
In your world
And one resting
In elfland
I walk amongst
The concrete flowers
And polluted jungles

With eyes open and wheels turning
I stroll along a path unknown

Away from that dream called the past
Away from that fairytale called the future
To the birth of everything
And the beginning of the universe

Here and now,
I found
The center of everything
In a blade of grass

XXXVI

There are times
Blossoming and thorny
When this mind
Becomes stretched thin
About to burst
And release its
Hidden life

There are times
When I come apart
At the seams
But never enough
To let go
Of this weird
Little me

There are times
When I cannot believe
In anything
So tragic as this
Silly and silent
Idea of a man
Who cannot find love

There are times
We work so hard
To be alone
That when it faces us
  The end
  The dark
We lose ourselves
But then there are times
When the terrible thing comes

The end

And in those moments
When I am about to burst
And lose what I cherish most
Then and only then

Do I lose something
Truly valuable
And only then
Do I smile

XXXVII

Descending
Into the space
Between birth
Spotted clouds
Of waking life
And dying
The end
Of my world
At last I see it
The fountain
The center
Of all that is
Cannot be
Touched by
The rational mind

Falling from
Surface to fear
I shake death
To the core
Of the lonely
Other one
That dwells
Within the light
Of my being
In the last
Moments of now
I can't help
But wonder

If the end is
Really that

For all my words
All my thoughts
All my life
Cannot explain
Away the fact
That death
Is not an
Experience
And here I
Hope that
In those last moments
Death will not find
Me still
Annihilated

XXXVIII

In this solemn final tower
Of days and endless weeks
     I approach
Slow and steady
Drawn on to my destiny

     I can see
     Ahead of me
In the dawn of a great ocean

An abyss of the warm and gentle unknown
In canyons and rivers

     The mind
Will not ruin this again
For around each of us
The stars swing
     Evenly

And here, now
The same unceasing wave
     Given to all
     Is rolling back
     Clear and void

Ready to be filled
With whatever I choose to be
Unrelenting
In every cycle
In every age

Ear to the earth
I must listen
To the voices, to the cries
And gather them
Together in a perpetual cup

And so, through me
The freedom I seek
Can find its meaning in others

And empower the voice
Of all those imprisoned

So then even this man
Rainy and calm
Can sing in the silence
Of his own failures

XXXIX

Together it goes
Hand in mind
The soft breaking light
That dims with the coming
Of autumn

In darkened rooms
        I wished
        For lightness

I wished to sing
        For no one

To sing without words
To see in myself
Those bright and fragile eyes
Awake and dying
To every little moment

Breaking Open the Heart

I wished for what felt so empty
     In those hours
Between the years of backward smiles
In this heavy clouded chest

In ignorance and haste
I sent myself running

For years, I drank
The question that love becomes

The question that turns
     Us inside out
And burns at the center of every word

I wished that for one day
I could see myself
Through the eyes of all the ones
And know my answer

But for now, it will be enough to sing
     A song for no one

And wish and hope that one day
     It will all be clear
     And that someday,
     I too will be the one

XL

Little by little
Thoughts cycle and
Cross each other
Coming from nowhere
Arising and passing away to
Where? Nobody knows

It does not matter
Because the light
Will always warm us
And reveal what is
And always was
       There

       How long
Has your own face
Waited in shadow?
       Each day
       Little by little
We build these walls

Around ourselves
Higher
With words
And thoughts that
Grown like weeds
And hide

From us the face
We wore before
Our parents met

Behind these clouds
The wind will move
And reveal the light

    That was
    And always is
    There

Who knows the destiny
Of my thoughts

Running away with me?

XLI

Glinting in the eyes
Of a lion lost in rain
A cold desert moon

XLII

How fast it leaves us
Speak of it in quiet shame
The end of romance

XLIII

On and on it goes
The music dances within
Listen it is gone

XLIV

Balance of the mind
In eyes that say goodbye
You will never know

XLV

Sinking forest sun
Tangled web of selfish thought
The leaves sway in time

XLVI

I don't understand
I don't know anything about it
These things that we dream

XLVII

Chimes sound in the deep
Wind blowing in foreign land
Life moves in water

XLVIII

In shadows and sand
Remembering nonsense past
Island in low tide

XLIX

Point to land and sea
Buddha dances in between
Lonely and is lost

L

Distant sound, still leaves
The plates are empty and gone
Waves are rolling in

LI

Pine needles falling
Contemplating distant shores
The light has returned

LII

The wheels go silent
The heart has stopped and fallen
It moves in darkness

LIII

In depth and shadow
It dwells and sleeps in laughter
The sound of wonder

LIV

You always see it
The hope we lose in secret
A smiling child cries

LV

Light turning inward
Here they sit and sit and sit
Buddhas, fools, and saints

LVI

Where are they going?
These people who think themselves
Growing like minds in spring

LVII

Grey skies; strange cities
Big minds with big hearts that lie
In glory, we march on

LVIII

Out here on the rim
Eternal turn of the wheel
Matters only to some

LIX

When horizons end
Where the flame turns to ashes
The sun wheel revolves

LX

Light peering through cloud
Long days wasted, wanting less
Breathe more than others

LXI

Between shade and light
Amongst the flowering vines
Summoning the rain

LXII

The end of all things
How little the smallest hand
Giving life to joy

LXIII

Legs to carry us on
Hands to fight against the loss
Hearts to swim upstream

LXIV

Paths that cross and leave
Loneliness in unity
The beautiful smile

LXV

Swelling pain rises
Nothing permanent but change
This body will die

LXVI

Why this persistence
The lingering mystery
There is no answer

LXVII

Abandoning pride
Walking the path of life
Holding myself low

LXVIII

Mind running away
The bottom of the bucket
Is still broken through

LXIX

Again, the sun came
To show the missing answer
Out in broad daylight

LXX

Swimming with the stream
Your disappearance as form
Only seasonal

LXXI

How can you be sad?
If there is no one to die
When the old shell falls

LXXII

Growing older still
Learning, growing, still breathing
Still just as stupid

LXXIII

Even the hardest thing
Can reveal in me the strength
I thought had died out

LXXIV

Tonight, I was brave
In her eyes, I found a hope
That conquers all doubt

LXXV

Butterflies inside
A smile that lightens the dawn
Of a growing me

LXXVI

How strange we all can be, rejecting
The grace that falls like rain
Of clouds in time, the darkened eye cannot see
What is lost in the idea of growing up

LXXVII

If only we could let go
Our silent wandering from day to day
With fist and teeth instead of smiles, tumbling
Through rolling sand, burning the soles of aching feet

LXXVIII

Beneath leaves that listen and stars that gaze
You are invited to drink the sweetest nectar
Within the shimmering reflection of a newly formed smile
Is waving like a distant lover, scattered across the pond

LXXIX

With roots that grow from within the belly
Knotted, entwined in deepening earth
The pain of a twisting motherhood is
Heavy with love that will not be severed

LXXX

At the end of rules and clever dreams
The doubt remains around the form
The speech that drips from hands and lips
Will never be the final right

LXXXI

Coming together upon the center
Lingering around the edge, you wander
Afraid to lose your footing, afraid to fall
Inwards, to a place we are not one

LXXXII

How deep the cut that cripples the day
That walks for me in lightened halls
Awkward, taking my steps away
In the place of another man's shadow

LXXXIII

Listen to sound in the universe
This loud passenger of the soul
Can only create noise
In the bed of silence

LXXXIV

The shade that dances past the shadow
Flutters in the wind of faith, in asking
Pass behind the veil
And beg the light to die forever

LXXXV

The fruit that blossoms from the hand
Moves without a darkened sea
If all the monuments could laugh
An empty soul would echo back

LXXXVI

Distracted, in this noisy mind
The river flows like any other
Carry away the hope and burden
Of the future always running

LXXXVII

Chasing my own shadow
I can see him smiling, just ahead
The dust circles from the center
Turning like the earth and moon

LXXXVIII

Standing atop the troubled day
The faded memory of sad dreams
Wait to reverse the anguish
With no when to welcome us home

LXXXIX

This stillness, heavy in the air, waiting
To push beyond itself, eager
With ecstasy in fingertips alive
In sensation, dense with awareness

XC

Beads of feeling pulse with will
The deepest touch of the mind
A body that dissolves in the breath
Like sand that rolls with muscle

XCI

The spine of a private world
Aligned in colored vision
Within the wheels grind and stop
Turned upside down and inside out

XCII

It just so happens, the who you think you are
Is someone, you would not believe
Look again, the stars are out
Who else could they be?

XCIII

Who is the center of all this?
The hearing ear, the tasting tongue
Biting your own teeth, thinking thoughts
No light without the eye

XCIV

Mistress, my ego is mistaken
The waning source
Convincing ourselves she isn't there
The emptiness behind the feminine black

XCV

There may come times in you
When the dry heaving brain
Is lost in what to do without
The word that glues the form to form

XCVI

The same something turns inside you
A love that moves the sun
Revolves evenly, the burning wheel
Beats the heart

XCVII

The inmost skin, pale in reflection
Against the real, ghost of me
The warm and tender flash of sight
Reveal the ache, longing for home

XCVIII

Dropping into the body
The space between seven breaths
Is all that we need
To see at last

CXIX

The meanings dance beyond the mouth
Parched, the lips about to speak
Escape the grasp of life imprisoned
In the miles of text behind us

C

The light receded
Past the gate of life
Weary in dream
I entered in alone
The veil drawn
Across the open silence
In all things
The magnetic center pulled
Towards its own star
Losing itself again
With sighing collapse
Of radial weight

The dark night
Of the one real drew inwards
Adorning face and name
To act the part
Of little me—
The tragic smiling fool
With reckless will
I plunged forth unafraid

For no less than the sun we give in turn
For this, the one chance to dance
The song of peace
Consuming planets
As the mighty scale
But here like all others
I faced the same
Rolling wave, splitting into equal drops
Of sight punched
In the fabric of what is

With open eyes
I saw this in the world

So grand the still beginning
Of all things
Yet sitting, these little hands, soft and young
The world was before
New and simple eyes
The stories intertwined
The roads rolled back
The way everything complicates itself
The stunning nonsense
Of a life untold
Nothing but the smallest things
In lightness
And ease the swaying
Stream of holy time
Like a whirlpool
Draining into the past
Tiny heart, beating so fast, little smile

Life in every detail, so clear, flowing
Gushing from the lips
Of speaking windows
Open into this—
The dream of a child
The same child in every tale
Every song
That speaks of smiles
And the bright shining dawn
The calm before
The eye of every storm

The meadows and
Open fields of childhood
Alight themselves
In each and every room
Making way for the simple act of play
The only real purpose
Behind the life
We all find in early days of freedom
With heartache and grace
I still remember
The rays of light
That pierced the looming cloud
The weight of the only others
     Closing in
Around the innocent gaze of my youth
But they could not have known
The life I lived
In silent wonder—
The miracles fell

Like tiny drops of windy rain
One by one
Revealing the truth
Even in ugliness
Even in the violent quaking anger
Even then the smallest hands
Can falter
And even then, a child
Can become old
The days become clear
The past like a door
Into all things defining
Lost and free

How do we even begin to understand?

How can a million small tales become words?

Where do we find
The courage to be brave
And look into our own eyes
Without shame?

Without regret?

The web reflects the drops of dew
Shining in their own image
Mirroring the end
Each containing the rest
Without judgment
The quiet failures we are given

The form, the name
Our center of the world
Everything as it should be
As it was
Shouting now
The fact that I alone knew
That I did it
I was responsible
For getting involved
It was always me
The beginning
The middle
And the end

Looking back
Nothing happened as it seems
Amazing, how many things were not so

There beneath the eyes
Of a watchful sun
I came, like all others
Into this world
Like a weed
Like every fountain of youth
I multiplied in every direction
Seeking the edges
Of what I call me
The light poured in
And around the edges
The muddied forms
Took shape and became clear

Then the sound, the giggle
The great surprise—
I AM, how certain we are
To know
The only thing to be sure of
In truth
The only thing
That will not pass away

In the long days to come
The low places
Of a mind still forming
Still in searching
Reacting, learning
That which is not me
And finding the strange
Limits of what is
I remember
I always do
Always

For although lonely
Years have come and gone
Although the face
In the mirror changed
The same simple
Truth will always persist
And only in the second childhood
Does the first one
The given one, reveal
The simplicity

The song
The great peace

All in all
The bodies pass behind us
They move, in and out
From days to this day
In front the paths
So often tripped over
Become alive
And open what remains
In the state of mind
All in common

All in all
The eye that wakes
To every dawn
Every sunbeam
That warms the skin, the face
Every face with soft cheeks
And lips, smiling
Smiling so sweetly
In the warmth
The light
That peers in through every room
In mornings
Shared, steam that rises
The dust in the air
The laughter
The cheers to push us onwards
Into the spaces shared

By friends and those
Mistaken faces
We call strangers
Racing to catch up
To that time long ago
When it left us
The shameful glances down
         And down
The shrugging shoulders
Shy heads turn
Away from the gaze
Fixated upon
The quaking mess
That does nothing
When lost

Friends come to show
The greatness in other
The best of ourselves
In spheres beyond us

How many do we forget?

How many leave us?

In every new face
Comes a new challenge
New responsibility to ourselves
To let go
To seek the strength
In weakness

And flow like water
Through the cracks of life

The more we give away
The more we get
The more we lose
The stronger we become
So strange
So complicated
To be sane

Turning back the mind,
Smoke and air and space
Alive with a life
Unknown in the child
But never fully lost
To the moments
Of connection
Lingering smiles and frowns
The two sides of every situation
How deep the thought
Receding into the heart
So fickle
Doing the best that we can
In all events
Like every story, forever
The island consciousness
Always alone
How hard we try to reach out
Beyond us
But each universe

Fated the same, still
The dream that one day
The spheres will cross us

What is the difference between stories?

What makes one of us a lonely ruin?

And the other
A colossus, striding
Through life
With ease and fury
Lingering
The outward breath
Of us little people
With our words
Sighing in gentle relief
To know it is alright
To be little

The dream to join
In union to something
Great and other and new
A love below
The fire in the belly
The ragging thought
Pulling in all directions
Always there
Desire, seeing the possibility
In every pair of passing eyes, staring
In every direction but ours, maybe

    One day
We will see into other worlds
So many worlds we live in, amphibious
Beneath the surface
Trying not to breathe
Not to break
The dark glass of our bubble
So often do we change our skin, to be
The careful player
In a careful world
A world so delicate
Where words carry
A dying weight
That no one can lift alone

Bearing in from all sides
The deep cold chill
The height of walls
That surrounds the dark ice
That vaults itself
Into walking bones
The heart projected outward
Always there
To meet the day
To shake the hand of pain
The quiet endings
The way it always starts
Every moment containing the collapse
Of a self, too young
To know the meanings
Embedded in every object, between

Space so full to the brim
Connecting all
From one to the other
The flow of night
The dark night we all pass through
In good time

How can the idea contain the whole?

How can one walk the path of life and fall?

From the heights
Of the greatest thing of all
The deepest part
Untouched by the chaos
The boiling surface of the lake, swimming
Around and around
In endless circles
Always to rise again
To the surface

Caged in states of mind
Corridors of thought
Yoked in stasis
Above the changing moods
Of a still familiar space, enclosing
The only passing whim
The miracle
The smells alive
With reminders, longing
To push through

To a new kind of life
A life that moves
In quiet ways behind
The kind of life
That festers in the open
The life that sees inside
While all the others
Struggle just to see

Mind open
Waves from all sides of me laugh
The gaze of others
Different from the core
That feels itself to be
All together
Different

A silver fog rolls in
All around me
The day changes
Just like all the others
But does not become night
There is the night
And we deal with it

Path and life coincide
The middle way

The cloud and the fire
Pillar of the sun
The open air, the light in everything

The deepest grass
The black smoke of the dawn
The ocean stretching
Before endless feet
Waves crashing in
From all sides of the dark
Oscillating the dying leaves of trees
In yellow, in orange, in red
Like paper of the
Cities far away
Fluttering and wasting
In the soft breeze

Catching ourselves
In the open updraft
Seeing into the depth of the timeless
Hour of our silent
Waking breath
And exhaling with us the shame, regret
For the life in us
Never before lived
Never given a chance
Now escaping
With the swift rush
Of moving wind, upward
And onward into the deep song, moving
With the self
Standing in light beside me

Foundations shake
The earth, silent water

Broken into shards
The reflecting moon
Seeing a face, your face, distorted, gone
Carried off into the crushing distance
Leaving you to stare
Into the silence
Into the impenetrable black void

Knowing now the harsh and empty feeling
This stranger in the heart
This I myself
Shining the light backward
Blinded again
By the body of the glinting red sun
The energy extending from all sides
Eternal body of my own universe

If I am my foot then I am the sun

The ceiling of stars
The cold descending
In open air that screams
Of the horizon
Clouding over
So many words and thoughts

About nothing, nothing at all

In dreams
It becomes clear and fades
Like everything else

The dark secrets that we lose together
Striking us down
At the height of our pride

I sound my final cry
Lost in the wild

The feet fall out from under the world
And the fire sweeps clean
The sounding earth
Eyes clenching to open
In disbelief
At the crumbling heartache
The stories
Still rolling back in one single open wave

The hands of God collide
In quiet rage
At last the light recedes
The gate of life opens

Before those who would dare not enter in

Grass and vines grow over the many paths
And we stand as one
In the open air

And sing together
Songs of the great peace

CI

Wake up! And leave all manner of things behind
And turn your gaze from god to humankind
Let us together look beyond the past
And see inside to face the truth at last
United depth since the beginning free
A maze indeed! But obvious to see!
The faithful weeds and flowers still remain
The fruit will rot, and still we are in pain
Together, we will break the rusted chains
And take it back, no more shall we restrain!
The path was walked, and still our leaders failed
Your blindness—the future for which you sailed
Nature will love our folly as it lies
Will wisdom come in time to cut the ties?
With laughter speak the language of the heart
I vindicate, you were God from the start

The God above of this we surely know
But what about the god that lies below?
Of people seen within the rightful place
Pointing at the truth of the hidden face
Saviors will die in worlds within our own
But ours to trace the savior still unknown
The One that dwells beneath the silent mind
Reveal to us the truth of human kind
Observe the way our systems fall apart
Our clever thought collapsing back to art
We send our worries out with us to space
Neglecting the home of the human race

But of the problems still we have to face
Not one so clear as finding our true place
The answer buried in our cultures mine
Staring us in the face the entire time

The chain of life connecting to the ground
Foundation, being, and universal sound

Presumptuous—the reasons we have found
To gaze at stars while we forget the ground
First, ask yourself this question, do not guess
On being God, could you be any less?
Ask of the earth from out of which you grew
Do I exist? Of course, this must be true
If not then ask yourself the very same
And hear the truth just as you speak your name

Of all things possible you must confess
Here logic fails to pass the reason test
Where all arises, all must pass away
And all that's born will surely die someday
Within the scale how clearly we can see
How opposites must coexist to be
Of all the answers that you know are true
Please ask, what is the opposite of you?

Respecting all we argue, all we call
The answer must be relative to all
In history, we see without the pain
That our pleasure could not have felt the same
In life, we seek one single end produced

To search for one and maximize its use
But how I ask can pleasure exist alone?
Maybe in pain the truth will still be shown
Through up and down and black and white we see
These opposites exist in unity

Throughout our past proud men have all ignored
The creed of nature each of us has stored
When minds are dull and break the sacred line
As victims to the illusion of time
The animals who cannot comprehend
At least they do not dread and fear their end
We fight and rage and suffer this for why?
No one knows what it really means to die

At the level our imperfections lie
Is harmony from one more level high
Knowledge becomes our prison and our place
Building walls in imaginary space
Perfection is the end we must attain
Or else, the struggle all will be in vain
Lucky for us the truth is plain and so
The path began ten thousand years ago

Heaven and hell are not your possible fate
But in the mind and of the present state
For years, we fight against the why and how
Not realizing, we create them now
The past and future are the biggest crime
It's now! Of course, there is no other time
Until the last in blindness we can see

The future is a time that will not be
Of all that's happened, ask—where has it gone?
In memory is all it stands upon
With equal eyes, in all there is the key
To open the door to eternity
In systems of belief we'll surely fall
But faith unlocks the answer here to all

To believe is to wish for and to wait
To cling to life and crush it for your fate
Belief can murder in the name of God
But faith would think that action mighty odd
Belief is fear converting to its name
But faith is trust accepting all the same
The truth of God no word will ever touch
But living it is possible as such

Poor modern man whose bleak and tortured mind
Sees patterns in nature hoping to find
The answer in science, ideas, and thought
Perceiving the world through what we've been taught
This net, this screen, creating the pride
That keeps us cut off and locked up inside
But life itself cannot be described
Despite all the ways in which we have tried
Becoming the slaves of compulsive thought
Mistaking symbol for reality sought
Content with the surface of life and desire
Infatuation and greed burn with fire
But quench the flame for truth is in our reach
If only we could practice what we preach

So go then! And look, take time and observe
Be still, be silent, all movement conserve
If one thing is sure, the search for what's true
Begins here and now and only with you
If truth doesn't exist, no statement is true
The ultimate question, not what, but who?
If only you knew, who in fact you are
The pain would be over, the truth not so far
Take back from the hand, observe in the mind
Subject and object are one in a kind
In rational thought where our error lies
The distinction of knower and known dies
When thinking and ego come to their end
No longer are concepts left to defend
The illusions we have of identity
In silence and stillness left now to see
The fact of existence, naked and odd
Expand and contract—the two hands of God

Since time immemorial, we have asked
Who am I? But still the answer is masked
Of what by knowing which all things are known?
What happens in death? Are we all alone?
How did existence come into being?
Why was I born, and what is life's meaning?
On what does the universe stand upon?
Where are its edges? And who is it on?

It's not this, not that, of God we say
Imprisoned in words, the truth will not stay
Not light, not being, nor love, or father

Not the creator, so do not bother
Only in experience can we know
When reality's seen, what's left to show?
The source and center, the unknowing mind
Lost in the desert of silence we find
The true final end of each human being
Discovering self, finally seeing
The divine is not separate or distinct
Neither can it die or become extinct
What was never born, cannot itself die
Our sun will die out, and so will the sky
But then I ask can space be destroyed?
Imperishable and unending void
Of course, it cannot! So, what then is space?
Your consciousness there for you to embrace
The stars, the cosmos, of course it is you!
What else could it be? You know this is true
The self, pure awareness, shines as the light
Within your own heart, surrounded by sight
The body, the soul, the heart, and the mind
At the end in death, the Self leaves behind

The world is the wheel of God turning round
Right here and now your identity found
The chains have been broken, so has the wall
But then again, they were not there at all
The path has been walked by countless a soul
The *Buddhas* they sing! You're already whole!
It's all up to you, the path will allow
The song of the void, liberation NOW!

This is a dream; this is a dream; this is a dream!
Hold to this,
And limitless oceans
Will sound their depths!

About the Author

Interested in religion and spirituality from childhood, Gregory has dedicated his life to embodying the Non-Dual Dharma traditions of Central Asia, India, China, and Tibet. Gregory has been writing poetry from an early age, considering it the ultimate means to communicate spiritual experience. Born and raised in the California, Bay Area, Gregory now resides in Portland, Oregon.

www.ingramcontent.com/pod-product-compliance
Lightning Source LLC
Chambersburg PA
CBHW071313090426
42738CB00012B/2689